UNIX®

SELF-TEACHING GUIDE

Wiley SELF-TEACHING GUIDES (STGs) are designed for first-time users of computer applications and programming languages. They feature concept-reinforcing drills, exercises, and illustrations that enable you to measure your progress and learn at your own pace. Other Wiley Self-Teaching Guides:

DOS 5 STG, Ruth Ashley and Judi N. Fernandez
INTRODUCTION TO PERSONAL COMPUTERS STG, Peter Stephenson
OBJECTVISION 2 STG, Arnold and Edith Shulman, and Robert Marion
QUATTRO PRO 3 STG, Jennifer Meyer
LOTUS 1-2-3 FOR WINDOWS STG, Douglas J. Wolf
PARADOX 3.5 STG, Gloria Wheeler
Q&A 4 STG, Corey Sandler and Tom Badgett
FOXPRO 2 STG, Ellen Sander
ALDUS PERSUASION FOR IBM PC'S AND COMPATIBLES STG, Karen Brown and Diane Stielstra
PFS:PUBLISHER FOR WINDOWS STG, Sean Cavanaugh and Deanna Bebb
PERFORM STG, Peter Stephenson
NOVELL NETWARE 2.2 STG, Peter Stephenson and Glenn Hartwig
MICROSOFT WORD 5.5 FOR THE PC STG, Ruth Ashley and Judi Fernandez
MICROSOFT WORD FOR WINDOWS 2 STG, Pamela S. Beason and Stephen Guild
WORDPERFECT 5.0/5.1 STG, Neil Salkind
WORDPERFECT FOR WINDOWS STG, Neil Salkind
SIGNATURE STG, Christine Rivera
MICROSOFT WINDOWS 3.0 STG, Keith Weiskamp and Saul Aguiar
WINDOWS 3.1 STG, Keith Weiskamp
PC DOS 4 STG, Ruth Ashley and Judi Fernandez
PC DOS 3.3 STG, Ruth Ashley and Judi Fernandez
MASTERING MICROSOFT WORKS STG, David Sachs, Babette Kronstadt, Judith Van Wormer, and Barbara Farrell
QUICKPASCAL STG, Keith Weiskamp and Saul Aguiar
GW BASIC STG, Ruth Ashley and Judi Fernandez
TURBO C++ STG, Bryan Flamig
SQL STG, Peter Stephenson and Glenn Hartwig
QUICKEN STG, Peter Aitken
COREL DRAW 2 STG, Robert Bixby
COREL DRAW 3 STG, Robert Bixby
HARVARD GRAPHICS 3 STG, David Harrison and John W. Yu
HARVARD GRAPHICS FOR WINDOWS STG, David Harrison and John W. Yu
NORTON DESKTOP 2 FOR WINDOWS STG, Gerry Litton and Jenna Christen
AMI PRO 2 FOR WINDOWS STG, Pamela S. Beason and Stephen Guild
EXCEL 4 STG, Ruth K. Witkin
QUARK XPRESS FOR WINDOWS STG, Kim and Sunny Baker

To order our STGs, you can call Wiley directly at (201)469-4400, or check your local bookstores. "Mastering computers was never this easy, rewarding, and fun!"

UNIX®

SELF-TEACHING GUIDE

George W. Leach

John Wiley & Sons, Inc.

New York ▲ Chichester ▲ Brisbane ▲ Toronto ▲ Singapore

THIS BOOK IS ONLY TO BE USED WITH LICENSED, VALID COPIES OF UNIX®. ANY OTHER USE CONSTITUTES FRAUD.

Library of Congress Cataloging-in-Publication Data
Leach, George W.
    UNIX : self-teaching guide / George W. Leach.
        p.   cm. -- (Wiley self-teaching guides)
    Includes bibliographical references.
    ISBN 0-471-57924-6 (paper :alk. paper)
    1. Operating systems (Computers)--Programmed instruction. 2. UNIX
(Computer file) I. Title. II. Series.
QA76.76.063L351993   92-30398
005.4'3--dc20   CIP

Printed in the United States of America
10 9 8 7 6 5 4 3 2 1

Contents Overview

To Hillary, I don't know where I would be without you

Contents

8 Communications, 155

9 Simple Shell Programming, 173

10 Other Shells and Tools, 197

11 System Management for Users, 209

Appendix A Alphabetic User Command Summary, 223

Appendix F Further Reading, 241

Index, 245

Preface

For nearly a decade UNIX has been the operating system of choice in the scientific and engineering communities, both in academia and industry. Over the past several years UNIX has been rapidly gaining popularity within the commercial sector as well, in areas such as stock trading, hotel reservations, and retail stores. The reason for this gain in popularity is that UNIX runs on many different brands and sizes of computers ranging from microcomputers to supercomputers and can be integrated with other, non-UNIX systems. A highly attractive feature of UNIX is the ability to change hardware with relative ease. The economics of positioning software systems to be moved onto newer, faster, cheaper hardware is hard to ignore.

About This Book

This book takes a user-oriented approach rather than a system-oriented approach. Many books will explain about a system in terms of its architecture and design and then cover the usage of the system within that framework. This book starts with the user, from the initial experience of accessing a system to some simple usage of the system, and then expands into more advanced topics. After you have had an opportunity to use the system, some of the finer points about UNIX will be explored.

To facilitate this approach, the book is organized into two parts. The first six chapters provide the basic introduction to the UNIX system. The material covered in these chapters allows you to quickly begin using UNIX in a productive manner. Topics are covered in sufficient detail to allow for basic usage, and then advanced topics follow. Chapter 1 provides you with background on the operating system. Chapter 2 discusses accessing the system and UNIX commands. Chapter 3 explores usage of the UNIX screen editor. Chapter 4 covers file manipulation. Chapter 5 expands the discussion to include the UNIX file system. And chap-

Trademarks

AT&T is a registered trademark of American Telephone and Telegraph.

BSD is a trademark of the University of California at Berkeley.

CHORUS is a registered trademark of Chorus Systems, Inc.

DEC is a registered trademark of Digital Equipment Corporation.

Hayes is a registered trademark of Hayes Microcomputer Products, Inc.

Hayes Smartmodem is a trademark of Hayes Microcomputer Products, Inc.

HP is a registered trademark of Hewlett-Packard Company.

IBM is a registered trademark of International Business Machines.

Intel is a registered trademark of Intel Corporation.

MOTIF is a trademark of the Open Software Foundation, Inc.

MS-DOS is a registered trademark of Microsoft Corporation.

OPEN LOOK is a registered trademark of UNIX System Laboratories, Inc.

OSF/1 is a trademark of the Open Software Foundation, Inc.

PROCOMM is a registered trademark of DATASTORM TECH-NOLOGIES, INC.

Sun is a trademark of Sun Microsystems, Inc.

SunOS is a trademark of Sun Microsystems, Inc.

TeleVideo is a registered trademark of TeleVideo Systems, Inc.

UNIX is a registered trademark of UNIX System Laboratories, Inc.

UNIX System V is a registered trademark of UNIX System Laboratories, Inc.

VT100 is a trademark of Digital Equipment Corporation.

WYSE is a registered trademark of Wyse Technology.

WY-85 is a trademark of Wyse Technology.

XENIX is a registered trademark of Microsoft Corporation.

X/Open is a registered trademark of X/Open Company Ltd.

Acknowledgments

I would like to thank my wife, Hillary, who, in addition to providing me with encouragement, understanding, and the quiet that allowed me to write this book, also played an active role in the production. Her experience as both a programmer and technical writer afforded me the luxury of a reviewer and editor sitting at my side.

I want to thank the reviewer supplied by Wiley for the thorough review of the manuscript and for numerous helpful suggestions.

Mike Wolfe of AT&T Paradyne (Largo, FL) also took the time and trouble to review the manuscript and provide input to this project.

I would also like to thank Gerald Cohen of GE Software and Consulting (Livingston, NJ) for the use of a machine and for being a good friend in a time of need.

UNIX®

SELF-TEACHING GUIDE

Introducing UNIX

Before getting started with using UNIX, you should learn a bit about where UNIX came from. It didn't start as a conscious effort to produce a product, but began as a grass roots effort to improve the inventors' work environment. This chapter provides you with some background information on the UNIX operating system. In this chapter you'll learn about:

▲ UNIX history

▲ UNIX design

▲ UNIX today

What Is UNIX?

UNIX is an operating system. Technically, it is a general purpose, multiuser, multiprocessing, interactive, time-sharing system—that's a mouthful! Put more simply, an operating system is a layer of software that sits between you and the hardware of the computer. Its job is to manage the resources of the system—both hardware and software—and to provide the user with access to these resources. In a multiuser environment, this can be a complex task. The resources that the system manages include the central processing unit, or CPU, memory, disks, terminals, printers, files, and services. In a sense, the operating system acts as a traffic cop, enabling users to get work done without interfering with each other.

UNIX is also a general purpose operating system that can be used for a wide variety of application areas. There are other operating systems that are geared toward very narrow application areas, such as managing the flight of the space shuttle or operating robots on an assembly line. UNIX can support more than one user at a time. And each user can be performing multiple tasks, called processes, at the same time.

The Origins of UNIX

UNIX is the brainchild of a handful of computer scientists at AT&T Bell Laboratories in Murray Hill, New Jersey. The impetus for developing the system, as the story goes, confirms the age old adage that necessity is the mother of invention.

In the late 1960s, Bell Laboratories was involved in a joint project with General Electric and the Massachusetts Institute of Technology to develop an operating system called MULTICS. MULTICS was an ambitious interactive, time-sharing system designed during the age of punch cards! While many interesting design issues arose out of the project, it proved to be too costly for Bell Labs and in 1969 a decision was made to pull out of the MULTICS project.

The staff members at Bell Labs who had worked with MUL-TICS had grown accustomed to its interactive environment. Thus, a new operating system was born—a scaled back version of MUL-TICS jokingly called UNICS. The name UNICS evolved into UNIX.

The Origins of UNIX

The History of UNIX

UNIX may never have grown beyond the small research group within Bell Labs that developed it for their own use; however, two events put UNIX on its course toward wider acceptance within Bell Labs. First, the research group proposed to develop a text processing system for UNIX in order to justify the purchase of a more powerful machine; second, the Bell Labs Patent Office needed a text processing system. The patent office selected UNIX over all of the other commercial systems. UNIX now had its first user community and with it a source of continued funding for its development.

In the early 1970s, the C Programming Language was developed by Dennis Ritchie of Bell Labs so that UNIX could be ported to new hardware platforms. The first version of UNIX written in C was developed in 1973. At this time, word spread both within Bell Labs and throughout academia about the work being done on UNIX. Consequently, a demand for making UNIX available to organizations outside of Bell Labs appeared. However, being a regulated monopoly, AT&T was restricted from selling UNIX commercially. So UNIX availability was limited to universities for educational purposes.

The UNIX operating system came in source code form, which encouraged much experimentation and led to numerous versions of the system within Bell Labs and outside of the Labs. The most significant external version of UNIX was developed at the University of California at Berkeley and is known as the Berkeley Software Distribution, or BSD. BSD UNIX is now used at thousands of universities throughout the world and was the basis for a number of vendors' commercial versions of UNIX that were created during the 1980s. The same AT&T research organization that originally developed UNIX and C is still actively involved in operating systems and programming language research to this day. Since the breakup of the Bell System in 1984, AT&T has been free to sell UNIX commercially. The version of UNIX that is available commercially from AT&T is called System V.

UNIX is also unique in that it is the first operating system to be written primarily in a high-level, portable language. Other operating systems such as MULTICS were written in a high-level language, but UNIX is the first truly portable operating system. Being written in a high-level language makes the software easier to understand than other systems written in proprietary assembly languages. This facilitates porting the system to new hardware with minimal effort. Applications can be written in such a way as to provide easy portability to any UNIX system. The user can therefore purchase any hardware that offers UNIX as an operating system, and with such hardware, the user can move applications to it with a minimum of effort. This is still a radical departure from the days of being locked into a vendor for all hardware and software needs. The rise of UNIX is responsible for what today is called Open Systems.

UNIX Today

UNIX evolved during the 1970s and the 1980s as new features were demanded by users and as research in operating systems produced new mechanisms for improving performance and capabilities. The UNIX system of today, while basically the same as early UNIX, has many more features.

In the late 1980s, AT&T struck an agreement with a couple of other companies, most notably Sun Microsystems, in an effort to bring together the most important commercially available versions of UNIX: AT&T's System V, Sun Microsystems', Berkeley-based SunOS, and Xenix, which is a PC version of UNIX. The end goal was to merge the versions into AT&T's System V and make it available on platforms from PCs, to workstations, to larger computers. This version is System V Release 4.0, which has been available for over a year, and is now in its third version from UNIX Systems Laboratories (USL).

Today we have various standards and user groups. There is POSIX. There is X/Open. There is OSF/1 and System V. There are the graphical user interfaces, Open Look and Motif. It can become very confusing. One thing is for sure: UNIX has gained enough popularity to warrant the attention of those who would like to see it go away, namely those companies who have profited in the past from locking their customers into their system. Within Bell Labs, the research editions of UNIX continue to evolve. Over the past number of years, smaller machines have been able to run UNIX that support graphics.

The Design of UNIX

The original UNIX design was based on simple, well-thought-out concepts, most of which were borrowed from other operating systems. There are a few main components that make up UNIX: the file system, process management, and the command interpreter. While each element of the system has its own role and responsibility, they work well together, as you shall soon see.

Getting Started

Now that you know a bit about UNIX's history, it's time to get started. The first steps are to gain access to the system, become familiar with your new surroundings, and perform some simple tasks. In this chapter, you'll learn about:

- ▲ **Accessing UNIX**
- ▲ **Configuring a terminal**
- ▲ **Using a modem**
- ▲ **Logging in**
- ▲ **Passwords**
- ▲ **The shell**
- ▲ **Simple commands**
- ▲ **The environment**
- ▲ **Logging out**

Accessing UNIX

How you access UNIX depends upon the configuration of your particular computing system and your physical proximity to the machine. It could be as simple as turning on your terminal, or it could be as involved as powering up and booting a personal computer or workstation. You might have to use a modem, or know how to connect to the computer through a terminal server or some other network device. Whatever your particular situation, you'll need to figure out which are the necessary steps that will connect you to the UNIX system. The next five sections may or may not apply to your environment. Select the sections that do apply, and ignore the others until you need them some time in the future.

Accessing UNIX with the Console

If you're the only person using a personal computer that's running UNIX, then you'll have exclusive use of the system console, which is directly connected to the machine. If the machine is not powered on, then turning it on will initiate the booting of the UNIX system. A number of messages appear on the screen as the booting of the system proceeds. They convey copyright notices, the UNIX version the system is running, and other information pertaining to the configuration of the system. Once that process is complete, the login prompt appears on the screen:

```
login:
```

At this point you're ready to login to the system. You may proceed to the section called, "Logging In."

Configuring a Terminal

If you're working with a terminal, or a PC equipped with terminal emulation software as part of a communications package—either directly connected to the computer or using a modem—you'll need to make sure that the terminal or terminal emulator is set properly for accessing UNIX. Terminals can be configured to work with a wide variety of computers and operating systems.

Most modern terminals allow you to modify the terminal set-up through the terminal itself. Check for a key marked Set-Up on your terminal. Pressing it produces a menu of options to select from by using function keys, arrow keys, or a combination of both. The manufacturer's user guide specifies how to configure your terminal.

Communications software for PCs running MS-DOS, such as Procomm, provide a terminal emulator that will allow the PC screen and keyboard to act like a typical terminal for the purpose of communicating with another computer. Furthermore, these communications packages also allow for the terminal emulator to be configured much in the same way as a terminal. Even better, most packages allow for multiple configurations to be stored and tied into specific phone numbers so that dialing a phone number will automatically set up the terminal emulator appropriately. Check the User's Manual of your favorite PC communications package for details.

Some terminal parameters deal with items such as how many lines are on the screen (typically 24), how wide is each line (typically 80 characters), does the cursor blink or is it solid, is the screen background dark or light, and so on. For these types of parameters you needn't do anything. The default settings will work. You may want to experiment with some of them and choose those that appeal to you. The parameters that are most important are those that deal with the communications set up. These parameters dictate how the terminal will communicate with a machine—via a direct cable connection, or over a dial-up link with a modem. If they do not match what the computer expects, you may get garbled communications, or no communication at all!

TIP

Some terminals support a printer port in addition to a communications port. Both ports will require configuring for communications. Make sure when setting up your terminal to communicate with UNIX, that you configure the right set of parameters for the communications port.

Communications speeds vary depending upon the devices on either end of a communications link. The unit of measure for data communications speed is called *baud*. The most common values that terminals support are 110, 300, 1200, 2400, 9600, and 19200 baud. Most terminals that are connected directly to a computer over a cable will run at speeds of 9600 baud or even higher. The same is typically true of terminals connected to a terminal server or other network device. Modems can support a wide variety of speeds as well, but typically 1200 or 2400 baud is the speed for a dial-up link. Not only do you need to know the maximum speed that your modem can support, but you also need to know the maximum speed that the modem you are dialing can support. The two must be in agreement. Often, you'll have to adjust the speed before placing phone calls on a number of different computers.

TIP

The speed setting on your terminal might be a single parameter, or it might have one for Receive and another for Transmit. If the latter is the case, make sure the two are set to the same value.

Table 2.1 shows a list of the remaining terminal parameters and typical values that pertain to data communications when accessing a UNIX machine. It's not important to understand their purpose in data communications at this point. It's simply important that they're set to the appropriate values. It should be noted, however, that there may be some variation based upon the particular machine with which you are trying to communicate.

TIP

Some of these parameters go under different names for different types of terminals. For example, Full Duplex communications are achieved on some terminals by setting the Echo parameter to OFF; on others there is a Duplex parameter whose value must be set to FULL. Once again, the terminal user's guide is the place to check parameters for your particular brand of terminal.

▼ *Table 2.1. UNIX Terminal Settings*

Parameter	Value
Data Bits	7
Parity	Even
Duplex	Full
Handshake	XOFF
Stop Bits	1

Directly Connected Terminals

Once the terminal is properly configured, and the configuration has been saved, simply press **Return** or **Enter** repeatedly until the login prompt appears:

```
login:
```

Should this fail, check the cables. They may be loose. Then make sure that the terminal is in Line mode and not Local mode. It might be a switch, or a key on the keyboard that sets the mode of your terminal. Or it might even be a parameter that is set through your terminal's setup. No matter what the mechanism you need to use, make sure that Local is OFF, or Line is ON.

Once you access the login prompt, you're ready to login to the system. You may proceed to the section called "Logging In."

Using a Modem

Configuring the communications port for the terminal or terminal emulator, in effect, configures the modem as well, assuming, of course, that the modem is connected to the communications port of the terminal. For PCs with emulators, the emulator software must be set to the same communications port that the modem's cable has been connected to, typically COM1. Make sure that the phone line is connected to the modem and the wall jack. Then make sure that both the terminal and modem are powered on.

At this point, the terminal and modem are connected and you're ready to issue commands to operate the modem from the terminal. The standard set of modem commands are borrowed from Hayes Smartmodem and are known as the Hayes Command Set. Virtually every modem on the market can support it. There are a number of commands that can be issued to a modem, but to dial a computer, you only need to know one.

TIP

Before attempting to dial a number with your modem, you may want to make sure that your modem is connected to your PC or terminal and functioning properly. You can do this by simply entering AT.Then press Return **or** Enter. **The modem should respond with an** OK **on the screen. If when you type** AT, **nothing appears on the screen, check the cable from the terminal to the modem, and make sure the modem is turned on. If you see a** NO CARRIER **message, make sure the phone line is plugged into the modem and the phone jack.**

You can send a command to dial the desired phone number by entering **ATDT#######** (where each # is a digit in the phone number); then press **Return** or **Enter**. All commands to the modem must have the prefix **AT**. The **DT** indicates that the modem should Dial(**D**) using Touch-Tone(**T**) Dialing. If Touch-Tone Dialing isn't available in your area, simply drop the **T** to get Rotary Dialing. Try both and listen to the sounds from the modem as it dials the number. If you've ever used a rotary phone, you'll recognize the sound. The phone number should contain all the digits necessary to place a call to the desired destination. For example, if you must dial an access code to get an outside line, typically a **9,** you can prefix the phone number with the code. The same is true when dialing a 1 and an area code to place a long-distance call.

TIP

When dialing a long-distance number insert a comma (,) between the 1 and the area code. This will cause a short delay between the 1 and the area code to allow time for the modem to receive the long-distance dial tone before sending the area code. Humans can't possibly dial fast enough to cause a problem, but modems can!

When the modem finishes dialing the number, you'll hear ringing through the modem's speaker. If you don't, look for a volume control on the modem and raise the volume. When the modem on the receiving end of the call answers, you'll hear a high pitched series of tones. The terminal's screen will display a message indicating that you're connected. If we dialed the phone number 555–5555 in this manner, the screen would appear as follows:

```
ATDT5555555<CR>
CONNECT 1200
```

Press the **Break** key several times until a prompt appears. If the modem you dialed into is directly connected to a UNIX machine, you'll eventually see the UNIX prompt:

```
ATDT5555555<CR>
CONNECT 1200
<Break><Break><Break>
login:
```

If you don't get the UNIX prompt, then there are a number of possible explanations. First, if you get a different prompt, you may have dialed into some intermediate device such as a terminal server. In that case skip to the next section on network devices. If you get nothing at all, continue to press **Break** until you do get something. If you get nonsense characters, then perhaps one of the terminal parameters is set improperly. Check them and try again. If the parameters are okay and you still get garbled characters on the screen, you may have a noisy phone line. Disconnect the modem by turning the power off. Turn it on again, and try dialing again.

You're now ready to login to the system. You may proceed to the section called, "Logging In."

Using a Network Device

In larger organizations a terminal server or some other type of network access device may sit between your terminal and the computer. The reason for this type of arrangement is to allow any terminal access to any computer on the network rather than attaching terminals to a specific machine. In addition, modems may be attached to such a device, thus allowing remote users to dial a single phone number to access different machines.

When you turn on your terminal, or establish a dial-up connection with a modem, you will be connecting to a network device rather than the actual computer. Accessing a UNIX system in this situation requires that you know the command the device needs to establish a connection to a machine, and the name of the machine you wish to access.

Most network devices display some sort of prompt at the least. Some display a message that indicates the type of device. A menu of options or commands might be displayed. Typically, help is available to guide you with these devices. At the prompt, enter either a question mark, **?**, or a help command, **help** or **h**. This produces a list of valid commands. Sometimes you can get help with specific commands by issuing a help command followed by the command name. For example, the **telnet** command allows you to remotely access a machine. Simply type **telnet machine-name**. The command sets up the connection between the terminal server and the machine over a network and presents you with status messages regarding the connection, the machine to which you are connecting, and the normal UNIX login prompt:

```
> telnet alpha<CR>
Connecting to alpha
Connected to alpha
UNIX System V R.4 (alpha)
login:
```

If there's a problem, a message appears indicating that the communication couldn't be established:

```
> telnet alpha<CR>
Connecting to alpha
telnet: connect: Connection timed out
>
```

It could be that the machine you're trying to connect to is down; or, if the name is incorrect, the network device won't be able to locate the machine. The messages you see might vary, but their purpose won't.

TIP

You might be asked to enter a password that allows you to issue commands to the device. If a password is required, you must ask your system administrator about it.

If you're using a network device, then there should be a system administrator who's responsible for keeping everything running smoothly. You might need to check with your system administrator concerning the commands, the machine name, and if necessary, to obtain a password to access the device itself.

Logging In

Once you've accessed the UNIX system, you might see messages on your screen regarding the organization to which the machine belongs, and possibly warning messages regarding use of the machine. In this age of cracking into computers this has become a necessity.

The item of interest to you on the screen is the login prompt, which is the mode of communication between you and the system indicating that the machine is waiting for you, or someone else, to attempt to login. The login prompt will appear as follows:

```
login:
```

In order to enter UNIX, you need a login id or *login* for short. In addition, you might need a password the first time you log into UNIX. A login (alternate names include: account, user id, user name, or login name) usually consists of one to eight lowercase letters and digits. The login is the means of identifying a specific user on a UNIX machine. Typically the user is allowed to select a login. So select one that uniquely identifies you. For example, I might choose **gwl** as my login. I could've just as easily chosen others such as **gleach**, **george**, or a nickname.

Once the login prompt is displayed, UNIX waits patiently for you to enter your login using the keyboard. Notice that as you enter the characters, they appear on the screen. UNIX reads the characters and echos them back to you on the screen. Once you've entered your login, press **Return** or **Enter**. After providing UNIX with input, you'll need to press **Return** or **Enter** in order to tell UNIX to act upon what you have entered. Notice that after pressing **Return** or **Enter**, the cursor returns to the first column and advances a line.

The next two sections deal with the different prompts that appear, according to your particular system. The third section deals with a prompt that you'll see, sooner or later. If you're anxious to start using UNIX, read the sections that pertain to the prompts you see on your system. However, you might want to read all of the sections to familiarize yourself with all the prompts.

Password

The next prompt you see is for a *password*:

```
login: gwl<CR>
password:
```

If you don't know the password, then contact your system administrator. Password protection is like a lock on a door. The password is like the key that opens the door to access your login. It is a security mechanism that is a must in a multiuser environment like UNIX. If the system doesn't prompt you for a password, that means that you currently don't have one, which means that your login is wide open to anyone who knows what your login is! Shortly you'll learn how to set up a password for your login, or to change an existing password.

Again, UNIX patiently waits for you to type in your password and end the input with a press of the **Return** or **Enter** key. Notice as you type your password that the characters you type with the keyboard don't appear on the screen as they did when you entered your login. The cursor remains in place until you press **Return** or **Enter**. Why? To ensure that someone looking over your shoulder can't "steal" your password and access to your login.

At some time you might mistype either your login or password. Or perhaps you might forget your password. When you enter a login or password that is incorrect, UNIX will deny you access to the system. Should this happen, you'll see the following sequence of messages:

```
login: gwl<CR>
password: <CR>
login incorrect
login:
```

Notice that no information is provided to help you figure out which part, the login or password, UNIX didn't like. This is another security precaution to make it more difficult for someone to break into the system. If you mistype your password or login, simply try again. If you can't remember your password, then you'll have to ask your system administrator to get rid of the current password so you can login. Don't forget to give yourself a new password! You'll learn how to do this later in this chapter.

Once you've successfully entered your login and password, the next prompt you see depends upon whether you are working from a terminal that is connected to a specific machine or one that can be connected to any machine using a modem or other device.

Terminal Type

UNIX is capable of supporting a wide variety of terminals. On systems where terminals are hard-wired to specific ports on the machine, the terminal type can be preset by UNIX. If you're accessing UNIX over a modem, a terminal server, or a network connection, UNIX won't know what type of terminal you're using. So the system asks you:

```
Term:
```

The prompt you see might be slightly different, but it will ask you for a **Term** or **Terminal Type** entry. Enter the terminal type that is appropriate for your terminal, or for the terminal emulator you're using. There are so many different types of terminals available from vendors that it would be impossible to list them all. A few of the more common terminals and their corresponding terminal types are presented in Table 2.2.

▼ *Table 2.2 Popular Terminals and Terminal Types*

Terminal Model	Terminal Type
DEC VT100	vt100
WYSE WY-85	WY85
Sun Workstation	sun
TeleVideo Model 925	tvi925
Hewlett Packard 2621p	2621

If you're unsure of your terminal type, and can't find out from a local expert, then use **vt100**. Most terminals support this terminal type because it's extremely basic.

The Shell

Finally, after entering your login, password, and possibly a terminal type, you may be presented with some greeting messages and/or other information. At this point, you've reached the UNIX command interpreter, more commonly known as *the shell*. The shell prompt is typically a character such as a dollar sign, **$**, or percent sign, **%**; however, on some systems the shell prompt contains the machine name followed by a dollar sign or some other character. For example, the prompt may appear as:

```
alpha:
```

This type of prompt is useful if you have logins on multiple UNIX machines, so that you know which one you're working with. Still another variation is:

```
alpha!gwl:
```

This prompt not only tells you what machine you're on, but also which login you're using. Yes, some people use multiple logins. Throughout this book, the simple dollar sign will be used as the shell prompt character. Later you'll find out how to change this symbol to suit your preferences:

```
$
```

Upon displaying the shell prompt, the shell waits for you to type in a command. Remember always to end a command by pressing **Return** or **Enter**; otherwise UNIX won't receive the command that you type. Once you enter a command, the shell executes the command, displays any output, and redisplays the prompt.

Some Simple Commands

Now that the scene has been set, you're ready to try your hand at some simple commands. Some UNIX commands are simple words or abbreviated forms of words that are descriptive of their action. Others are not so obvious. Many of the command names may seem unusual to you. They are holdovers from a time before video displays, when terminal speeds were extremely slow and keystrokes needed to be kept to a minimum. Some commands have options, others don't. Commands may or may not take *arguments*—entries that identify the items to be operated upon. In time you'll see examples of commands that exhibit all of these traits. The general format of a command line is the command name, followed by the options, and then the arguments:

```
$command -opt1 -opt2 . . . arg1 arg2 . . .
```

Alternatively, options can be combined, so that only one dash is necessary:

```
$command -opt1opt2 . . . arg1 arg2 . . .
```

The first command you need to learn is the **passwd** command. This command allows you to set a password for yourself if you don't currently have one, or to change the current password. Before examining the **passwd** command, you need to learn the rules for choosing your password. While these rules aren't enforced on all UNIX systems, following them will ensure that you choose a valid password for any UNIX system:

▲ A password should contain at least six characters but can contain up to eight.
▲ At least two alphabetic and one numeric or punctuation character must be included in the password.

Choose a password that's easy to remember, but not one that's easy to guess, such as a name and birthday or a relative's name.

TIP

It's better to use both upper- and lowercase characters in passwords so that guessing becomes even more difficult.

Now that you know how to choose a password, you can execute the command. Type passwd:

```
$passwd<CR>
```

Depending upon whether or not you currently have a password, UNIX may or may not prompt you for your current password:

```
Changing password for gwl
Old password:
```

At this point, you must enter your current password. Once again, as with the login sequence, UNIX won't display the characters you type on the keyboard. The reason UNIX requests that you enter your current password is to make sure that you, indeed, are the owner of the login.

If the password you enter is incorrect, then UNIX responds with the following message:

```
sorry
$
```

If you successfully enter the current password, UNIX prompts you for a new password:

```
New password:
```

After deciding upon a password, type it in at the prompt. Again, UNIX won't display what you type as you enter your new password. If the password you enter isn't valid according to the rules for forming UNIX passwords, one of several possible messages appears:

```
Password is too short—must be at least 6 digits
New Password:
Password must contain at least two alphabetic
```

```
character and at least one numeric or special
character
New Password:
```

Finally, if the new password conforms to the rules, then UNIX requests that you retype your new password:

```
Retype new password:
```

If the retyped password doesn't match the original new password, you will see the following message:

```
Mismatch—password unchanged
$
```

You'll have to invoke the **passwd** command again to change your password. The next time you login use this new password in order to gain access to the system. In either case, the **passwd** command has completed its work, and the shell prompt reappears as UNIX awaits another command:

```
$
```

CHECK YOURSELF

1. Which of the following are not valid passwords?
    wizard   me1
    uRL8   RuMyD8
    R2d2C3pO   john#5

2. Construct some potential passwords for yourself. Check them against the rules presented here.

3. Select one of these passwords and try to set it on UNIX.

ANSWERS

1. wizard has enough characters, but no numeric or special characters. me1 has too few characters. uRL8 has too few characters.

2. The possible answers are too numerous to list here.

3. Type the **passwd** command. If applicable, enter the old password. Then enter your new password twice.

Another simple command allows you to test your new password. It is the **login** command. This command allows you to login again, possibly using a different login:

```
$login<CR>
login:
```

At this point you can again log into the system. Your initial login session is disconnected by this command, so you're starting all over again. Assuming that you have a password, you'll be prompted for one:

```
login:gwl<CR>
password:
```

So far, the only commands you've seen concern your login and password. Now it's time to learn some commands that are useful for your everyday UNIX activities. The first such command is **date**, which reports today's date and the current time:

```
$date<CR>
Thr Jun 13 21:02 EST 1991
$
```

Because UNIX is a multiuser system, there might be other people on the system. The **who** command tells you who is on the system and when each person logged in:

```
$who<CR>
brad          tty01        Jun 13 10:07
hill          tty02        Jun 13 07:31
alm           tty05        Jun 13 09:30
brad          tty06        Jun 13 09:15
monica        tty13        Jun 13 08:06
jacob         tty10        Jun 11 12:46
gwl           tty12        Jun 13 07:35
$
```

The **who** command presents a list of logins, ordered by the second column, which is the tty line to which the login is attached. The term *tty* is derived from the old Teletype terminals of yesteryear. The date and time, which uses military time, indicates when each user logs in. Notice that there are two **brad** entries. There is no reason why a single login can't be used at the same time on two different terminals (tty lines). At some time you may wish to know who is currently on the terminal. The **who** command can be used with the arguments: **am i** to access this information:

```
$who am i<CR>
gwl             tty12           Jun 13 07:35
$
```

Another useful command is **echo**. **echo** takes input of one or more arguments and simply echos the arguments back to the screen:

```
$echo hello there<CR>
hello there
$
```

Notice that the arguments, **hello** and **there**, are separated from the command, **echo**, and from each other by blank characters. UNIX doesn't care how many blanks you use between arguments. It simply ignores the excess blank characters:

```
$echo hello     there<CR>
hello there
$
```

If you do want to preserve the blanks between **hello** and **there**, then you need to use quotes, ":

```
$echo "hello     there"<CR>
hello     there
$
```

While it may not seem very useful, **echo** comes in handy, as you shall see later on in the book.

Another command that works in a similar fashion to echo is the **banner** command. **banner** accepts arguments in the same manner that echo does, but echos them back in larger print, one argument per line. Figure 2.1 illustrates using **banner** with three arguments.

What if you want to print more than one word, including the blank on the same line? Then, you must put the two words together between a set of quotes, ", to form a single argument. This technique is shown in Figure 2.2.

▼ *Figure 2.1. Using banner with three arguments*

```
$banner one two three<CR>

 ####    #     #    ######
#    #   ##    #    #
#    #   # #   #    #####
#    #   #  #  #    #
#    #   #   ##     #
 ####    #    #     ######

#####    #     #    ####
   #     #     #   #    #
   #     #     #   #    #
   #     # ##  #   #    #
   #     ##  ##    #    #
   #     #     #    ####

#####    #     #    #####    ######   ######
   #     #     #   #     #   #        #
   #     ######   #     #   #####    #####
   #     #     #   #####    #        #
   #     #     #   #   #    #        #
   #     #     #   #     #  ######   ######
```

Another handy command displays a calendar for the current month:

$cal<CR>

```
         July 1992
     S   M  Tu   W  Th   F   S
             1   2   3   4   5   6
     7   8   9  10  11  12  13
    14  15  16  17  18  19  20
    21  22  23  24  25  26  27
    28  29  30  31
$
```

The **cal** command can also display the calendar for any month of any year, or the calendar for an entire year. Suppose you want to see which day your birthday falls on in 1993. If your birthday falls

▼ *Figure 2.2. Using banner with a quoted argument*

```
$banner "one two" three<CR>


  ####     #     #   ######     #####   #     #    ####
 #     #   ##    #   #             #     #     #   #    #
 #     #   # #   #   #####         #     #     #   #    #
 #     #   #  #  #   #             #     # ##  #   #    #
 #     #   #   ##    #             #     ##  ##    #    #
  ####     #     #   ######        #     #     #    ####


 #####     #     #   #####    ######   ######
     #     #     #   #     #   #        #
     #     #######   #     #   #####    #####
     #     #     #   #####     #        #
     #     #     #   #    #    #        #
     #     #     #   #     #   ######   ######
```

within the month of March, you would use the **cal** command with
the arguments **3 1993**:

$cal 3 1993<CR>

```
         March 1993
    S   M  Tu   W  Th   F   S
            1   2   3    4   5   6
    7   8   9  10  11   12  13
   14  15  16  17  18   19  20
   21  22  23  24  25   26  27
   28  29  30  31
$
```

By leaving out the month argument and simply supplying a
year argument, the calendar for the entire year is produced. Give
it a try.

Another command that you might find to be quite useful is
the **bc** command. The **bc** command allows you to perform arithmetic calculations. **bc** invokes an interactive program that you
continuously use until you wish to stop. When finished, simply
use a Control d **(^d)** to end the program. When used without any
options, **bc** performs integer arithmetic (no fractions):

```
$bc
3/2
1
^d
$
```

TIP

Control d (^d) isn't an arbitrary way of specifying the end of a program. In fact, it is the End Of Transmission (EOT) character and is used with many other UNIX commands as well.

When used with the **-l option, bc** performs decimal arithmetic, as opposed to integer arithmetic:

```
$bc -l
3/2
1.50000000000000000000
^d
$
```

The commands presented here should provide you with a general feel for how the system operates. Later chapters discuss families of commands that concentrate on a specific functional area of UNIX, such as working with files.

CHECK YOURSELF

1. Check the date and time.

2. See who is on the system.

3. Figure out what login you're using.

4. Check the calendar for this month.

ANSWERS

1. Enter the **date** command.

2. Enter the **who** command.

3. Enter the **who** command with the arguments **am i**.

4. Enter the **cal** command.

Correcting Typing Errors

By now you should have had ample opportunity to make plenty of typing errors. Perhaps you mistyped a login or password. Maybe you pressed the wrong key while entering a command. For example, you may have intended to enter the **passwd** command, but instead typed:

```
$paswd<CR>
paswd: Command not found.
$
```

Before pressing the **Return** or **Enter** key, you can correct your mistakes. This is called command–line editing. There are two characters that the shell interprets as editing commands. The pound sign, **#**, is for character deletion. When pressed, it deletes the preceding character. On many terminals the **Backspace** key has taken the place of **#**. To correct the mistyped command, type the **#** or press the **Backspace** key twice after the **d** in **paswd**. This will erase the **wd**. At this point, the command entry can be completed by typing **swd**.

If you type a long command line and wish to start all over again, there's also a line delete or kill character, the ampersand, **@**. When pressed, it deletes the entire line and leaves the cursor next to the prompt.

The Environment

The shell has some customization features that allow you to tailor the environment to suit your needs. Certain characteristics of your login environment are stored in shell variables that programs in the system make use of. The terminal type that you enter when you log in, or the one that the system sets for you, is stored in a shell variable. You're able to view the current contents of that variable and change it during the course of your login session. The name of the variable that contains the terminal type is **$TERM**. Notice that the name is in all uppercase letters and that it is preceded by a dollar sign, **$**. In order to query the shell for the contents of the variable, ask **echo** to display its contents by using the **$TERM** shell variable as an argument:

```
$echo $TERM<CR>
wy85
$
```

You need to supply the dollar sign, **$**, when requesting the contents of a shell variable. This enables the shell to distinguish the shell variable **TERM** from a character string argument **TERM**:

```
$echo TERM<CR>
TERM
$
```

You may also mix text with the shell variable:

```
$echo My terminal is a $TERM<CR>
My terminal is a wy85
$
```

To change the contents of a shell variable, set the shell variable to a new value by entering the variable name *without* the dollar sign, **$**, followed by an equal sign, **=**, and finally the new value. Do not leave blanks on either side of the equal sign, **=**:

```
$TERM=vt100<CR>
$
```

If this attempt to set your **$TERM** shell variable resulted in a message like:

```
TERM=vt100: Command not found.
$
```

this indicates that you're running a different shell than the one discussed here. If this is the case with your system, simply enter the command **sh** and attempt to set the **TERM** shell variable again. The **sh** command invokes the Bourne Shell, which is what is described here. Other shells will be discussed later.

Perhaps you would like to change the prompt character to something other than the dollar sign. This function is also stored in a shell variable, called **PS1,** or Prompt String 1. Try the following:

```
$echo $PS1<CR>
$
$
```

Now you can change it to something a bit more friendly:

```
$PS1=Command:<CR>
Command:
```

And to be a bit more polite:

```
Command:PS1='Command Please:'<CR>
Command Please:
```

Notice that the new value for **PS1** is surrounded with single quotes. You must treat it this way in order to pick up the blank between the two words. The same is true for any other shell variable. To change back to the original prompt character:

```
Command Please:PS1=$<CR>
$
```

In addition to built-in shell variables, you're free to create your own variables, assign values to them, and use them. All shell variables must start with either an alphabetic or underscore, _, character. You can then follow with more alphabetic or numeric characters. Using uppercase alphabetic characters is conventional, but you can also use lowercase characters when creating your own variables.

You assign values to your own shell variables in the same manner as you do for built-in variables. Perhaps you have difficulty remembering your phone number. Define a variable called **PHONE** and set it to your phone number:

```
$PHONE=555-1212<CR>
$echo $PHONE<CR>
555-1212
$
```

You can also set shell variables to commands so that when you try to examine the contents of the variable it executes the command. In order to do this, you must surround the command with backquotes:

```
$D=`date`<CR>
$echo The current date and time is: $D<CR>
The current date and time is: Fri Jun 14 01:15
EST 1991
$
```

The variables you create only last for as long as you are logged in. Upon your leaving the system, they disappear. After you learn a bit about editing files, you'll learn how to define and set your own shell variables and the shell's built-in variables, so that they will be present every time you login. Other built-in shell variables will be presented as you explore new features.

CHECK YOURSELF

1. Change your shell prompt string.

2. Create a new shell variable called **NAME**, set it to your name, and display its contents.

3. Set a new shell variable called **ME** to the appropriate command so that when you display its contents it causes the current login information to be displayed.

ANSWERS

1. Set the **PS1** shell variable using a command line similar to **PS1=enter:**.

2. **NAME="John Q. Public"**
   echo $NAME

3. **ME=`who am i`**
   echo $ME

Logging Out

When you finish working with UNIX for the day, it's a good idea to lock up your login. Failure to do so leaves your login wide open to any casual passerby who happens to sit down to your keyboard and screen. To do this, you need to log out of the system.

There are two different ways to log out of a UNIX system from the shell prompt. The easiest way is to enter **exit**. And the other method is to hold down the **Control** and **d** keys, **^d**, simultaneously. Although this is difficult to remember, this sequence of key strokes is used throughout UNIX, so you will become familiar with it. You needn't press **Return** or **Enter**. You're now disconnected from the system and have to login again in order to gain access.

Logging Out

QUICK SUMMARY

Command	Description
ATDT5555555	instruct a modem to dial a number
telnet	command to connect to a machine through a network device
login:	the UNIX login prompt
password:	the UNIX password prompt
Term:	a UNIX prompt for terminal type
passwd	change your password
date	display the current date and time
who	see who is on the system
who am i	find out what login you're using
echo	echo arguments to the screen
banner	create banners
cal	display a calendar
bc	calculator
$TERM	shell environment variable that contains the current terminal type
$PS1	shell environment variable that contains your shell prompt characters
exit	exit from the system
^d	exit from an interactive command or the system

PRACTICE WHAT YOU'VE LEARNED

These exercises provide practice logging into UNIX.

What You Should Do	*How the Computer Responds*
1. Access your system.	1. Displays the login prompt.
2. Enter your login.	2. Displays the password prompt.

What You Should Do	*How the Computer Responds*
3. Enter your password.	3. Might display some messages and a prompt for the terminal type. Eventually displays the shell prompt.
4. Use **date** to check the date and time.	4. Displays the date and time.
5. Use **who** to find out who is on the system.	5. Displays a list of the current logins on the system, along with the tty number, and date and time of login.
6. Use **echo $TERM** to check your terminal type.	6. Displays the terminal type.
7. Use **cal**, followed by month and year to check the day of week for the 20th of next month. For example, **cal 1 1992**.	7. Displays next month's calendar.
8. Change the shell prompt to display "May I Help You?" by modifying the shell variable: **PS1="May I Help You?"**.	8. Displays "May I Help You?" when the shell is waiting for you to enter a command.
9. Use **who** to find out whether anyone else has logged in since you last checked.	9. Displays a list of the current logins on the system along with the tty number and date and time of login.
10. Enter **PS1=$** to change the shell prompt back to the dollar sign.	10. Displays a dollar sign when the shell is waiting for you to enter a command.
11. Use **cal** to print the calendar for the entire year.	11. Displays the calendar for each month of the year.
12. Enter **banner I Luv UNIX** to create a banner that reads: "I Luv UNIX."	12. Displays "I Luv UNIX" in large print.

What You Should Do	**How the Computer Responds**
13. Use **login** to login again.	13. Displays the login prompt. Enter your login id and when prompted, your password.
14. Use **date** to check the date and time again.	14. Displays the date and time.
15. Use **exit** to logoff the system.	15. Displays the login prompt.

WHAT IF IT DOESN'T WORK?

1. If you're using a terminal and you see patterns that don't make sense, check the terminal parameters and make sure they're set properly. If you're using a modem to access the system, you may need to press the **break** key several times to get the login prompt. If you're using a modem and the situation continues, disconnect the line by powering it off, and try dialing again. You might just have a noisy phone line.

2. If you're prompted for a password and the system doesn't accept what you type, either you were provided with a default password and weren't told about it or you've forgotten your password. In either case, you should talk to your system administrator. If there's a default password, you can find out what it is, and try again. If you forget what your password is, have the system administrator delete it, login, and reset it using the **passwd** command.

3. If any command results in a "Command not found" message, you may have mistyped the command. Remember that there are special characters that allow you to edit a command line before pressing **Return** or **Enter**.

Editing Files
with **vi**

This chapter lets you work with some of the basic features of the *visual editor*, **vi** (pronounced vee-eye), which you'll use to create and modify your own files. Additional features of **vi** will be covered in Chapter 7. In this chapter, you'll learn about:

- ▲ **Files and filenames**
- ▲ **The vi editor**
- ▲ **Editing modes**
- ▲ **Editing a file**
- ▲ **Inserting text**
- ▲ **Cursor motion**
- ▲ **Deleting text**
- ▲ **Searching**

Files and Filenames

A file is the basic means of storing information on most computers. Think of a file as a potentially endless piece of paper upon which you may write just about anything that the computer keyboard allows you to type. There are a number of commands provided in UNIX for manipulating files. However, first you'll learn how to create and modify the contents of a file. Then, in the next chapter, you'll concentrate on what you can do with the files.

There are several different types of files in UNIX. In this chapter, you'll learn about regular files. For the duration of this chapter, these types of files will be referred to as "files." Later, as other types of files are introduced, their distinctions will be clarified. A file is simply a collection of characters. The valid characters that you may store in a file come from the ASCII character set. ASCII is short for American Standard Code for Information Interchange. Virtually all computers, from PCs to supercomputers, and all video display terminals and keyboards are capable of working with this code. The only exception to this rule is the IBM mainframe, which has a code of its own. Thus any character that is represented by a key on your keyboard can be used in a file. Files are used for writing documents, composing messages, organizing lists, creating phone directories, and for many other purposes .

Before examining what goes into a file, you'll learn about the rules for naming files in UNIX. They are few and simple. First, the length of a filename may be anywhere between 1 and 255 characters. Second, filenames may be composed of any of the valid characters that your keyboard provides, except for the slash, /, which has a special purpose that will be discussed later. Special characters, such as the character delete, #, and line delete, @, must be preceded by a backslash, \, character, which tells the shell not to interpret the character as a delete character. Other special characters that should be preceded by a backslash when used as part of a filename are the asterisk, *, question mark, ?, square brackets, [and], and even the backslash character, \. You will see what these characters are used for later when you examine the shell in more detail.

TIP

Applying a backslash to the slash character in order to include it in a filename won't work! Try it with *vi* and see.

CHECK YOURSELF

1. Which of the following are not valid filenames?

    ```
    my_data        YourData
    1              %
    xyz/           Bills!
    ```

2. List some types of information that can be stored in a file.

ANSWERS

1. Only xyz/ is not valid due to the slash (/) contained in the name.

2. Names and phone numbers, addresses, letters and memos, electronic mail messages, and so on or just about anything you would like to save and access can be stored in a file.

The **vi** Editor

vi is a UNIX command that requires you to use a completely different set of commands in order to manipulate the contents of a file. Appendix C provides a handy summary of all the commands that are available in **vi**: Until you become comfortable with the basic commands, you might want to keep a copy of the Appendix nearby for quick reference when editing files.

vi can be used to edit an existing file or to create a new file. In either case, simply type the command, **vi**, followed by one or more filenames. To create a new file, simply select an unused name to be used with **vi**. To modify an existing file, provide **vi** with the name of the file you wish to edit. For now, you'll be creating new files.

Editing Modes

There are two primary modes of operation in the **vi** editor. They are command mode and input mode. *Command mode* means that **vi** is ready to receive and act upon a **vi** command, such as delete, insert, append, and move commands. Also, while in this mode, you can maneuver through the file using a number of different techniques. Most commands are initiated by pressing a single key, or possibly two keys simultaneously. When issuing a command, the character or characters that the key represents normally are not displayed on the screen (there are exceptions that you'll see shortly)—the action the command directs simply takes place. For example, certain keys must be pressed in order to advance to another screen or page of a file. When requested to do so, **vi** simply responds to the command.

Some of the commands put you into *input mode*. When in this mode, everything you type on the keyboard goes directly onto the screen and into the working copy of the file. When you're done entering text, you press the **Esc** key to end the input mode and return to command mode. An *editing session* is a series of command mode and input mode instructions in which you switch between modes in order to get work done.

TIP

Some terminals provide a status line at the top or bottom of the screen. Normally, on these types of terminals you can tell when you're in input mode because there's a message on the status line, such as INS.

The input commands and the **Esc** key are the two mechanisms for switching between the two modes. It's extremely important to understand the difference between the two modes and to recognize which mode you're in at all times; otherwise, you can inadvertently cause the wrong action to occur. For example, if you're in command mode, but think you're in input mode, when you start typing text, you could type a key that causes a command to execute, such as delete! This could cause you to lose one or more lines. This is quite common, even among experienced **vi** users. But don't panic—there's a mechanism you'll learn about that can undo what you've done, should you find yourself stuck in such a situation.

Editing a File

To create a file from scratch, select a filename that doesn't currently exist. Then type **vi** followed by the filename. For example, create a file to store a simple phone book using **vi**. Call the file **phone**:

```
$vi phone<CR>
```

After pressing **Return** or **Enter**, you will see a blank screen with a tilde, ~, character in the first column of each row, the name of the file with the designation [New file] in the lower left corner of the screen, and the cursor, positioned in the upper left corner of the screen (Figure 3.1). The number of rows that appear on your screen depends upon your monitor. There are typically 23 or 24 rows.

Input some text with **vi** by typing an **a** for append. Notice that the **a** didn't appear on the screen. Remember: When you issue a

▼ *Figure 3.1. Initial vi Screen for a New File*

```
[ ]
~
~
~
~
~
~
~
~
~
~
~
"phone" [New file]
```

command to **vi**, it simply takes the action you requested. Now start typing what you would like to enter in the file. As you type, the characters appear on the screen and the cursor advances to the right across the line. When you want to move to the next line, press **Return** or **Enter**. Type several lines. For example, try inputing some names with phone numbers so that the screen appears something like Figure 3.2.

If you want to put some blank lines in the file, just press **Return** a number of times. Otherwise, it's fine to leave the cursor at the end of the last line you typed. When you're done entering information, hit **Esc** to exit the input mode. The cursor moves back one character over the last character you entered.

TIP

vi **provides an option to display an** INPUT MODE **message that appears at the bottom of the screen when you're in the input mode. To turn this option on, you must use the** :set showmode **command within** *vi*. **You'll see how to do this later.**

You're now back in command mode. Finish your editing session by saving your new file. Press the uppercase **ZZ** twice

▼ *Figure 3.2. vi Screen While in Input Mode*

```
        Bradley G. Futia    813-555-5555
        Marion Leach        908-555-5555
        Cynthia Topfer      212-555-5555
        Vincent Futia       201-555-5555[ ]
        ~
        ~
        ~
        ~
        ~
        ~
        ~
        "phone" [New file]
```

(hold down the **Shift** key and press two **Z**'s). The information is saved by **vi** to the file called **phone**. The screen then appears like Figure 3.3.

Cursor Motion

The basic steps for modifying existing text are (1) move the cursor to the desired position, and (2) issue a command. Before learning about the commands, you'll learn how to move the cursor.

The simplest motions to learn are the four directional motions: up, down, to the right, and to the left. If your keyboard supports arrow keys, and the terminal type was set properly when you first logged in, you can use the arrow keys to move in the horizontal and vertical directions within **vi**. If there are no such keys on your keyboard, or if the terminal type you use doesn't support the arrow keys, then there's an alternative set of keys that you can use. Table 3.1 displays these keys along with the corresponding arrow keys and their direction of movement.

Table 3.2 illustrates examples of cursor movement with a series of before and after snapshots of a few lines from a file that only

▼ **Figure 3.3. Saved New File with** vi

Bradley G. Futia	813-555-5555
Marion Leach	908-555-5555
Cynthia Topfer	212-555-5555
Vincent Futia	201-555-5555

~

~

~

~

~

~

~

"phone" [New file] 4 lines, 112 characters

▼ *Table 3.1.* vi *Cursor Movements*

↑	k	move upward one line
↓	j	move downward one line
←	h	move left one character
→	l	move right one character

contains names. The current cursor position is indicated by surrounding the character with the square brackets, [and].

The **Backspace** key moves the cursor to the left. The **Return** or **Enter** key advances the cursor to the beginning of the next line in the downward direction, and the **space bar** moves the cursor to the right. A series of single key depressions moves the cursor one character or line at a time. Holding the key down moves the cursor continuously to a desired position. The only exception to this

▼ *Table 3.2.* **Example Cursor Motion Commands**

Before	You Type	After
[B]radley G. Futia Marion Leach Cynthia Topfer	l	B[r]adley G. Futia Marion Leach Cynthia Topfer
B[r]adley G. Futia Marion Leach Cynthia Topfer	jj	Bradley G. Futia Marion Leach C[y]nthia Topfer
Bradley G. Futia Marion Leach C[y]nthia Topfer	k	Bradley G. Futia M[a]rion Leach Cynthia Topfer
Bradley G. Futia M[a]rion Leach Cynthia Topfer	h	Bradley G. Futia [M]arion Leach Cynthia Topfer
Bradley G. Futia [M]arion Leach Cynthia Topfer	j	Bradley G. Futia Marion Leach [C]ynthia Topfer

rule is the **Return** or **Enter** key. But be careful; if the system is acting slowly, you can get ahead of yourself by holding a key down for too long. The cursor might end up positioned beyond where you want it to go.

These simple cursor movements are all you need to position the cursor anywhere you like within a file in **vi**.

Cursor Motion

CHECK YOURSELF

1. Use the editor to create a new file.

2. Switch to input mode.

3. Type in a few lines of input.

4. Switch to command mode.

5. Practice moving the cursor in all four directions.

6. Save your work and end the editing session.

ANSWERS

1. Enter the **vi** command, followed by a filename.

2. Depress the **a** key to append.

3. Type in a few lines of information.

4. Press the **Esc** key.

5. Use the arrow keys and/or the **j, k, h,** and **l** keys.

6. Enter **ZZ**.

The file you've been experimenting with isn't even large enough to fill a screen. But files can grow quite large. It's tedious moving from the top of a large file, several hundred lines down, using only the down arrow key or the **j** key over and over again. For larger jumps in positioning the cursor, there's another set of commands to use.

You can page or scroll in the vertical direction. Paging causes the screen to clear and then displays the next or previous screen of text in the file. To page forward, use <^f>. To page backward, use <^b>. If your terminal supports the **Page Up** and **Page Down** keys, then use them. Scrolling gives the appearance of the screen moving in a line-by-line fashion, up or down, to display more text. To scroll, use **^u** for up and **^d** for down. When scrolling, you only get a portion of a new screen, not the entire new screen that paging provides. Give them both a try to see which you prefer.

That should be enough to get you started. There are additional **vi** commands for moving about on a single line or to specific places within a file. But these will be discussed in Chapter 7.

Inserting Text

To input a new line within a file, first, position the cursor anywhere on the line above where you wish to input the new line. Press the **o** key, for open. A line will open up underneath this position and the cursor will be moved to the beginning of this new blank line. You're now in input mode: Enter as much text as you like. To enter multiple lines, simply end one line by pressing the **Return** or **Enter**. A new line will open up underneath the current line where you may continue to enter text. When you've entered all of the new text that you want, don't press **Return** or **Enter**. Press the **Esc** key instead. This takes you out of input mode and puts you back into command mode. Figures 3.4 through 3.7 illustrate how to use this method to add a new line to the file.

What if you want to input a new line above the very first line in the file? The procedure described above won't work! You can

▼ *Figure 3.4. Initial* vi ***Screen with an Existing File in Command Mode***

[B]radley G. Futia	813-555-5555
Marion Leach	908-555-5555
Cynthia Topfer	212-555-5555
Vincent Futia	201-555-5555

▼ *Figure 3.5.* vi *Screen After Issuing the o Command*

```
Bradley G. Futia          813-555-5555
[ ]
Marion Leach              908-555-5555
Cynthia Topfer            212-555-5555
Vincent Futia             201-555-5555
```

▼ *Figure 3.6.* vi *Screen after Entering a New Line*

```
Bradley G. Futia          813-555-5555
Monica L. Leach           813-555-5555[ ]
Marion Leach              908-555-5555
Cynthia Topfer            212-555-5555
Vincent Futia             201-555-5555
```

▼ *Figure 3.7.* vi *Screen after Depressing* Esc *Key*

```
Bradley G. Futia          813-555-5555
Monica L. Leach           813-555-555[5]
Marion Leach              908-555-5555
Cynthia Topfer            212-555-5555
Vincent Futia             201-555-5555
```

use the **O** command to open a new line above the current line. Figures 3.8 through 3.11 illustrate how to input a new line at the top of the file using this mechanism.

vi provides many mechanisms like the **o** and **O**—commands that come in pairs. They both open a new line. However, each opens a new line in a different position relative to the current position of the cursor. The **o** opens under the current line, while the **O** opens above the current line. In many cases, the one to use is up to you. However, when dealing with the first or last line in a file, you absolutely need both types of open commands.

▼ *Figure 3.8.* *Initial* vi *Screen with an Existing File in Command Mode*

[B]radley G. Futia	813-555-5555
Monica L. Leach	813-555-5555
Marion Leach	908-555-5555
Cynthia Topfer	212-555-5555
Vincent Futia	201-555-5555

▼ *Figure 3.9.* vi *Screen after Issuing the O Command*

[ ]	
Bradley G. Futia	813-555-5555
Monica L. Leach	813-555-5555
Marion Leach	908-555-5555
Cynthia Topfer	212-555-5555
Vincent Futia	201-555-5555

▼ *Figure 3.10.* vi *Screen after Entering a New Line*

Howard Bernier	516-555-5555[ ]
Bradley G. Futia	813-555-5555
Monica L. Leach	813-555-5555
Marion Leach	908-555-5555
Cynthia Topfer	212-555-5555
Vincent Futia	201-555-5555

▼ *Figure 3.11.* vi *Screen after Depressing Esc Key*

Howard Bernier	516-555-555[5]
Bradley G. Futia	813-555-5555
Monica L. Leach	813-555-5555
Marion Leach	908-555-5555
Cynthia Topfer	212-555-5555
Vincent Futia	201-555-5555

Often you want to input text in the middle of an existing line. There are commands that allow you to do this as well. First, you need to move the cursor to the desired position on the line where you wish to enter the new text. Again, there are two paired commands from which to choose—**a** to append and **i** to insert. The append command begins input after the current cursor position, while the insert command begins input before it. Tables 3.3 and 3.4 show the two different ways to accomplish this task.

Why do you need two ways to do this? Well you don't, most of the time. When you input new text in front of the first character on a line, you must use **i**. And, likewise, when you input text after the last character on a line, you must use **a**.

Inserting Text

CHECK YOURSELF

1. Edit the file created in the last Check Yourself.

2. Add a new line to the bottom of the file.

3. Add a new line to the top of the file.

4. Add a new line to the middle of the file.

5. Add a new word to the beginning of a line.

▼ **Table 3.3. Inserting Text with** *i*

Before	You Type	After
[J]im Leach	lll	Jim[ ]Leach
Jim[ ]Leach	i	Jim[ ]Leach
Jim[ ]Leach	my	Jimmy[ ]Leach
Jimmy[ ]Leach	<Esc>	Jimm[y] Leach

▼ **Table 3.4. Inserting Text with** *a*

Before	You Type	After
[J]im Leach	ll	Ji[m] Leach
Ji[m] Leach	a	Jim[ ]Leach
Jim[ ]Leach	my	Jimmy[ ]Leach
Jimmy[ ] Leach	<Esc>	Jimm[y] Leach

6. Add a new word to the end of a line.

7. Add a new word in the middle of a line.

8. Save your work and end the editing session.

ANSWERS

1. Enter the **vi** command, followed by a filename.

2. Use the **j** key to move to the bottom of the file and use the **o** key to open a new line. Finish with the **Esc** key.

3. Use the **k** key to move to the top of the file and use the **O** key to open a new line. Finish with the **Esc** key.

4. Use the **j** key to move to the middle of the file and use either the **o** or **O** key to open a new line. Finish with the **Esc** key.

5. Move to the beginning of the line and use the **i** command to insert a word. Finish with the **Esc** key.

6. Move to the end of the line and use the **a** command to append a word. Finish with the **Esc** key.

7. Move to the middle of the line and use either the **a** or **i** command to append or insert a word. Finish with the **Esc** key.

8. Enter **ZZ**.

Deleting Text

Deleting text is accomplished by moving the cursor to the desired position in the file and issuing one of the delete commands. You may delete single characters, words, a line, or a group of lines, depending upon which command you use.

To delete a single character, move the cursor over the character to be deleted and press the **x** key. The character the cursor is positioned over will disappear and the characters to the right of the cursor will shift one place to the left to fill in the gap. To delete multiple characters (right up to the end of the line if you wish), continuously press the **x** key. Table 3.5 presents an example of using this capability.

If you use the **x** key to delete the last character on a line, the cursor will then move back one space to the new last character. If you delete all the characters on a line in this manner, a blank line results. In order to delete the line, you must use a different command.

Deleting Text

To delete a single line, position the cursor anywhere on the line to be deleted and press the **d** key twice (**dd**). The line is deleted and all lines underneath it shift up one line to fill in the gap. The cursor ends up at the beginning of the line underneath the deleted line. To delete multiple lines, continuously use the **dd** command. Table 3.6 illustrates how to use **dd** to delete a line.

CHECK YOURSELF

1. Edit the file used in the last Check Yourself.

2. Delete some characters on a line.

3. Delete a line.

4. Delete another line.

5. Save your work and end the editing session.

ANSWERS

1. Enter the **vi** command, followed by a filename.

2. Move to a line using **j**; move over to some characters on the line using **l**; use **x** to delete a few of them.

3. Move to another line using **j** or **k**. Delete the line using **dd**.

4. Move to another line using either **j** or **k**. Delete the line using **dd**.

5. Enter **ZZ**.

▼ **Table 3.5. Deleting Text with** *x*

Before	You Type	After
[J]immy Leach	lll	Jim[m]y Leach
Jim[m]y Leach	x	Jim[y] Leach
Jim[y] Leach	x	Jim[ ]Leach
Jim[ ]Leach	<Esc>	Ji[m] Leach

▼ *Table 3.6. Deleting a Line with* dd

Before	You Type	After
[B]radley G. Futia		B[r]adley G. Futia
Marion Leach	l	Marion Leach
Cynthia Topfer		Cynthia Topfer
B[r]adley G. Futia		Bradley G. Futia
Marion Leach	j	M[a]rion Leach
Cynthia Topfer		Cynthia Topfer
Bradley G. Futia		Bradley G. Futia
M[a]rion Leach	**dd**	[C]ynthia Topfer
Cynthia Topfer		

Searching

Often when editing a file, you know what you want to change, but perhaps you don't know where it is in the file. To locate the desired word or line that you wish to work with, you can visually inspect a screen full of the text and page forward until you find what you're looking for. While this strategy works well with small files, it's ineffective when working with large files. Searching in this manner takes some time and proves to be a strain on your eyes. Why not let **vi** do the work for you?

There are two basic search commands, / and **?**. When issuing a search command, determine in which direction from your current position you wish to start, forward or backward. To search forward, type a slash, /, followed by the string of characters, called the search string. To search backward, use a question mark, **?**, instead of a slash, /. When you type the / or **?**, it appears in the lower left corner of the screen, so do the characters that you type after it. This allows you to see what you're typing and provides you with the opportunity to correct mistakes that you make while typing the command. If you make a typing mistake, you can backspace and correct it. And, yes, the line delete character, @, also works. Figure 3.12 displays such a search string prior to executing the search.

To issue the command press **Return** or **Enter**. **vi** responds in one of two ways: If the search string exists somewhere in the file, following the direction you specify, the cursor is then positioned at the first character found in the search. If the search string isn't found, then the message "Pattern not found" is displayed in the lower left portion of the screen and the cursor is returned to its position prior to issuing the search command. In Figure 3.13, the search found a match and moved the cursor there.

Perhaps the string that's found matches the search string, but isn't exactly what you're looking for. In this case, rather than retyping the same search string in order to look again, simply issue the **n** command to find the next occurrence of that string. Figure 3.14 shows the result of applying this command after the first search found a match.

If the next occurrence of the search string isn't on the same screen page, **vi** automatically positions the cursor in the appropriate place in the file and displays the new page on the screen. You may use **n** at any time to apply the most recently used search string. For example, you can specify a search string, find its first occurrence, page forward three pages, and then use **n** to continue searching. Furthermore, you can use **n** indefinitely. Once the search reach-

Searching

▼ *Figure 3.12. Specifying a Search String*

```
    Howard Bernier          516-555-5555
    Bradley G. Futia        813-555-5555
    Monica L. Leach         813-555-5555
    Marion Leach            908-555-5555
    Cynthia Topfer          212-555-5555
    Vincent Futia           201-555-5555
    ~
    ~
    ~
    ~
    ~
    ~
    ~
    /Futia[ ]
```

es the bottom of the file, or top if you are searching backward, it wraps around to the opposite end to continue the search.

Undo

vi allows you to undo the effects of the most recent modification command issued. This is an important capability. If you mistakenly delete 100 lines, you don't want to lose them! Nor do you want to exit **vi** without saving the changes you make in order to avoid losing those 100 lines! Undo can help. Simply press the **u** key. The deleted lines reappear.

You can also use **u** in cases where you input information and then change your mind. After leaving input mode and entering command mode, simply type **u**. All of the input disappears. Table 3.7 displays this capability.

TIP

If you're not sure whether you're in input mode or whether you issued an erroneous command, simply press Esc a few times and then press u.

▼ *Figure 3.13. Result of a Successful Search*

Howard Bernier	516-555-5555
Bradley G. [F]utia	813-555-5555
Monica L. Leach	813-555-5555
Marion Leach	908-555-5555
Cynthia Topfer	212-555-5555
Vincent Futia	201-555-5555
~	
~	
~	
~	
~	
~	
~	
/Futia	

▼ *Figure 3.14. Result of Using n to Search Again*

Undo

Howard Bernier	516-555-5555
Bradley G. Futia	813-555-5555
Monica L. Leach	813-555-5555
Marion Leach	908-555-5555
Cynthia Topfer	212-555-5555
Vincent [F]utia	201-555-5555

~
~
~
~
~
~
~
/

CHECK YOURSELF

1. Edit the file used in the last Check Yourself.

2. Search forward for a pattern.

3. Search backward for a pattern.

4. Delete a line.

5. Undo the delete.

6. Input a new line.

7. Undo the input.

8. Save your work and end the editing session.

ANSWERS

1. Enter the **vi** command, followed by a filename.

2. Enter a slash, /, followed by the pattern to be searched for, and press **Return**.

3. Enter a question mark, **?**, followed by the pattern to be searched for, and press **Return**.

▼ **Table 3.7. Inserting Text, Then Undoing it with** u

Before	You Type	After
[A]l Moshi	**ll**	Al[ ]Moshi
Al[ ]Moshi	**i**	Al[ ]Moshi
Al[ ]Moshi	**bert**	Albert[ ]Moshi
Albert[ ]Moshi	**<Esc>**	Alber[t] Moshi
Alber[t] Moshi	**u**	Al[ ]Moshi
Al[ ]Moshi	**u**	Al[b]ert Moshi
Al[b]ert Moshi	**u**	Al[ ]Moshi

4. Enter **dd.**

5. Enter **u.**

6. Using either **o** or **O**, enter a new line and press **<Esc>**.

7. Enter **u.**

8. Enter **ZZ.**

Leaving vi

When using **vi**, you're working with a *temporary copy* of the file. When you leave **vi** using **ZZ**, you're requesting **vi** to save the changes to the file, and then quit the editing session. At any time during the editing session, you can request **vi** to save changes, but not exit the editing session. This is accomplished using the **:w<CR>** command for write.

If you decide to leave **vi** without making changes to the file, then you need to issue the *quit* command. You quit by typing, **:q<CR>**. Notice that when you issue a **vi** command that begins with a colon (**:**), the cursor moves to the lower left corner of the screen, and what you type becomes visible (Figure 3.15).

The command isn't issued until you press **Return** or **Enter**. Once you press **Return** or **Enter**, if you've not made modifications to the text, **vi** exits without making changes to the file, and returns you to the UNIX prompt.

▼ *Figure 3.15. Directing* vi *to Quit*

```
Howard Bernier          516–555–5555
Bradley G. Futia        813–555–5555
Monica L. Leach         813–555–5555
Marion Leach            908–555–5555
Cynthia Topfer          212–555–5555
Vincent Futia           201–555–5555
~
~
~
~
~
~
~
:q
```

If you make changes to the temporary file, but don't save them to the actual file, and then you issue the **:q<CR>**, **vi** warns you that you made changes. A message replaces the **:q<CR>** in the lower left corner of the screen, and the cursor is positioned in the text where it was when you first issued the **:q<CR>** command. See Figure 3.16 for an example.

If you don't want to lose the changes, you can issue a different command to save them. Otherwise, if you do want to quit, issue the **:q<CR>** command with an exclamation mark on the end, **:q!<CR>**.

TIP

You can periodically save your work by issuing a :w<CR> **command every once in a while. You can also save the temporary file to a different filename by issuing a** :w filename<CR> **command.**

CHECK YOURSELF

1. Edit the file created in the last Check Yourself.

2. Quit **vi**.

3. Edit the file again.

4. Add some lines.

5. Quit without saving the changes.

6. Edit the file again.

7. Add some lines.

8. Save your work and end the editing session.

ANSWERS

1. Enter the **vi** command, followed by a filename.

2. Use **:q** to quit.

3. Enter the **vi** command, followed by a filename.

4. Use **o**, **O**, **a**, or **i** to add some lines.

5. Use **:q!** to quit.

▼ *Figure 3.16. Message from vi When Trying to Quit with Changes*

```
[H]oward Bernier 516–555–5555
Bradley G. Futia   813–555–5555
Monica L. Leach    813–555–5555
Marion Leach       908–555–5555
Cynthia Topfer     212–555–5555
Vincent Futia      201–555–5555
~
~
~
~
~
~
~
No write since last change (:quit! overrides)
```

6. Enter the **vi** command, followed by a filename.

7. Use **o, O, a,** or **i** to add some lines.

8. Enter **ZZ**.

QUICK SUMMARY

Note: All but the first command are **vi** commands, which means that they can only be used within the **vi** editor, and aren't available in other parts of UNIX.

Command	Description
vi	invoke the **vi** editor
i	insert before current cursor position
a	append after current cursor position
o	open a line below current line
O	open a line above current line
<Esc>	exit input mode, switch to command mode
ZZ	save file and exit **vi**
↑ or k	move upward one line
↓ or j	move downward one line
← or h	move left one character
→ or l	move right one character
<Backspace>	move left one character
<Enter>	move to the first character of the next line
^f	page forward
^b	page backward
^u	scroll up
^d	scroll down
x	delete current character
dd	delete current line
/	search forward for pattern
?	search backward for pattern
n	repeat last search command
u	undo last change
:set showmode	set **vi** show mode on
:set noshowmode	set **vi** show mode off
:w	write to the file
:q	quit **vi**

PRACTICE WHAT YOU'VE LEARNED

Editing a .profile

When you first login on a UNIX system, certain environment variables and parameters are set to default values. However, you can set up a special file that tailors the environment to suit your specific taste. This file is named **.profile**. If you don't have a default, **.profile**, create your own.

In Chapter 2 you learned about some of the *shell variables* that are available with UNIX. Rather than setting them each time you login, you can set the default definitions in the **.profile**. The following is a sample **.profile.** Use **vi** to create the file, or if it exists, to modify it.

Some shell variables that you can set are shown below. Set your **PS1** shell variable either to your machine name, your login, or a combination of both. The **echo** causes a prompt to be printed on the screen. The **read** reads what you type into the shell variable **TERM**. The **export** makes sure that the values given both to **PS1** and **TERM** are made available to all programs that you're authorized to execute:

```
PS1="alpha $ "
echo "Enter Terminal Type:"
read TERM
export PS1 TERM
```

What You Should Do

1. While in your HOME directory, edit your profile by executing **vi .profile**.

2. If a new file, use **i** for insert. Otherwise skip to step 9.

3. Type **PS1="alpha $ "** replacing alpha with your machine name or some other prompt. Press **Return**.

How the Computer Responds

1. The **vi** screen appears. Either an existing file appears or the bottom of the screen indicates that this is a new file.

2. The screen doesn't change, but anything you type is input on the screen. You're now in input mode.

3. The line you type is visible on the screen.

What You Should Do	*How the Computer Responds*
4. Type **echo "Enter Terminal Type:"** and press **Return**.	4. The line you type is visible on the screen.
5. Type **read TERM** and press **Return**.	5. The line you type is visible on the screen.
6. Type **export PS1 TERM** and press **Return**.	6. The line you type is visible on the screen.
7. Press the **Escape** key.	7. **vi** exits the input mode and enters the command mode.
8. Use **ZZ** to end your **vi** session.	8. **vi** saves the file and exits to UNIX. The UNIX prompt is displayed. Skip the remainder of the steps in this section.
9. Use **PS1** to locate the line where **PS1** is set.	9. Cursor advances to the line containing **PS1**.
10. Use the **cw** command, possibly more than once, to change the current value of the **PS1** shell variable to the value you would like.	10. **vi** reflects the changes made to the line.
11. Use **/read TERM** to locate the line where **TERM** is read.	11. Cursor advances to the line containing **read TERM**.
12. Check for an **echo** immediately preceding this line. If you don't like the prompt, change it using **C**. If none exists, use **O** to open a new line and follows steps 4 and 7.	12. **vi** reflects the changes made to the line.
13. Use **export** to locate the line where **export** is located.	13. Cursor advances to the line containing **export**.

What You Should Do	**How the Computer Responds**
14. Make sure that both **PS1** and **TERM** appear on such a line. Note that there may be more than one, so use **n** to search for the next **export** if necessary.	14. **PS1** and **TERM** should be on a line with **export**.
15. If you can't find one or both, use **i** to add them to an existing line with **export**. Follow steps 7 and 8.	15. Variables are added to the **export** line as needed.

WHAT IF IT DOESN'T WORK?

1. **vi** indicates that you only have read access to the file or that you are not allowed to write. Check to make sure you're in your HOME directory.
2. **vi** can't locate PS1 in step 9. Open up a new line using **o**. Perform steps 3 and 7.
3. **vi** can't locate read TERM in step 11. Open up a new line using **o**. Perform steps 4, 5, and 7.
4. **vi** can't locate export in step 13. Open up a new line using **o**. Perform steps 6, 7, and 8.

Working with Files

In the last chapter you learned how to create your own files. This chapter focuses upon the UNIX commands for working with files. In this chapter, you'll learn about:

- ▲ Listing files
- ▲ Copying files
- ▲ Moving files
- ▲ Removing files
- ▲ Viewing files
- ▲ Printing files

Listing Files

Listing the names of all files available to you is accomplished by using the **ls** command. **ls** provides you with a simple list of all filenames in a single column in alphabetical order. For example, assume you're working on a book in which each chapter is placed in a separate file. With **ls** you can list all of the files you've created:

```
$ls<CR>
Part_1
Part_2
app_a
bio
four
one
table
three
two
$
```

Notice that the files are listed, uppercase, alphabetic characters first, followed by those files that begin with lowercase characters. By default, the **ls** command lists filenames in the following ASCII character set order:

```
! " # $ % & ' ( ) * + , - . /
0 1 2 3 4 5 6 7 8 9
: ; < = > ? @
A B C D E F G H I J K L M N O P Q R S T U V W X Y
Z
[ \ ] ^ _ `
a b c d e f g h i j k l m n o p q r s t u v w x
y z
{ | } ~
```

If the number of files exceeds the number of lines available on the screen, you can't view all of the files in a single column. To view a multiple-column listing, simply append a **-C** to the command:

```
$ls -C<CR>
Part_1    bio    four    table    two
```

```
Part_2   app_a  one   three
$
```

To arrange the list of files horizontally across each row rather than vertically down each column, use the **-x** option:

```
$ls -x<CR>
Part_1 Part_2  bio       app_a     four
one    table   three     two
$
```

To override the default alphabetical order, and arrange the list of files in order of modification from most recent to least recent, use the **-t** option:

```
$ls -t<CR>
four
two
three
table
one
app_a
Part_2
bio
Part_1
$
```

To arrange the list of files according to the last date and time of modification, and present the list in multiple columns, combine the **-C** and the **-t** options:

```
$ls -Ct<CR>
four    three    one      Part_2    Part_1
two     table    app_a    bio
$
```

TIP

Most commands allow for a great deal of flexibility in specifying options. For example, ls with the C and t options could be used in any of the following formats: ls -Ct, ls-tC, ls -C -t, and ls -t -C. However, there are exceptions. Check the *UNIX Reference Manual* to check your options.

Again, the files are ordered vertically down each column. Thus, the way to read this list is that **four** is the most recently modified file. **two** is the next most recently modified file, **three** is next, and so on.

To search for specific files, provide **ls** with a list of the files you're looking for, and separate them with one or more blanks. For example, perhaps it's been a while since you last worked on your book and you're not sure whether you've created chapters one, two, and three:

```
$ls one two three<CR>
one
three
two
$
```

Despite the fact that the filename **two** precedes the filename **three** in the argument list given to **ls**, the output of the command is still in alphabetical order. When using **ls** with arguments, it's possible that some of the files you're looking for don't exist. In such a case, **ls** tells you:

```
$ls four five<CR>
five not found
four
$
```

You can tailor the output to suit your taste by combining options and filename arguments with **ls**. To request a list of specific files, arranged in order of modification time, and output the list horizontally, across the rows:

```
$ls -xt one two three four<CR>
four     two     three    one
$
```

A mistake that you can make with any UNIX command, not only **ls**, is to use the command with incorrect arguments. In this case, you receive an error message. For example, the following command line contains an illegal **-z** option:

```
$ls -z<CR>
ls: illegal option — z
usage: ls [-RadCxmnlogrtucpFbqisf] [files]
$
```

The preceding "usage" message displays all of the options that are available with the **ls** command and shows the format of the command. The square brackets **([ ])** indicate that providing **ls** with a list of filenames is optional. As you can see, there's quite a long list of options available with **ls**. Other **ls** options will be discussed in the next chapter.

Listing Files

CHECK YOURSELF

1. List the files available to you.

2. List the files with their modification times.

3. List the files in order of their modification times.

4. List the files in multiple columns.

5. List a specific file.

ANSWERS

1. Use the **ls** command with no arguments.

2. Use the **ls** command with the **-l** option.

3. Use the **ls** command with the **-t** option.

4. Use the **ls** command with the **-C** option.

5. Use the **ls** command with a filename.

Copying Files

Often you'll want to make a copy of an existing file and give it a new name. Why would you want to do this? Well, frequently you find that you need to create new files that are similar to existing ones. Rather than retyping information in a new file using **vi**, you can copy an existing file and then make changes using **vi**. To copy one file to another, use the **cp** command, followed by the filename of the existing file, and then the filename of the new file:

```
$cp four five<CR>
$
```

Two different files now exist, one named, **four,** and the other, **five,** both containing the same contents. However, they're separate files: Changing one has no impact upon the other. To convince you that a copy indeed was made, issue the **ls** command, and see that a different file listing results:

```
$ls<CR>
Part_1
Part_2
app_a
bio
five
four
one
table
three
two
$
```

WARNING

The order in which the filenames appear as arguments to cp **is important! The first argument is the file of which a copy will be made, while the second argument is the file that will be created from a copy of the first. If the order of the arguments gets mixed up, you may actually overwrite the wrong file. So be careful!**

TIP

Be careful with the name you choose for the second file with the cp **command. If you accidentally select the name of an existing file, UNIX will without warning overwrite that file with the new file being created by the** cp **command. If this happens, you can't retrieve the old file unless someone performed backups onto a diskette or tape.**

Moving Files

There are times when you want to move a file. Or perhaps you want to rename a file. For example, after creating the file **five**, you want to rename it **5**. This can be accomplished with the **mv** command:

```
$mv five 5<CR>
$
```

Using the **ls** command, you see the results of this command:

```
$ls<CR>
5
Part_1
Part_2
app_a
bio
four
one
table
three
two
$
```

Again, be careful entering the second filename with the **mv** command. **mv** moves the file from the first filename to the second and will destroy an existing file if it has the same filename as the second argument in the command.

Removing Files

To free up disk space, use the **rm** command to remove one or more files. Simply issue the **rm** command with a list of filenames separated by blanks. For example, to remove a single file, simply issue the command with a single filename:

```
$rm bio<CR>
$
```

Use **ls** to verify that the file was indeed removed:

```
$ls<CR>
Part_1
Part_2
app_a
five
four
one
table
template
three
two
$
```

To remove several files, use **rm** followed by a list of filenames:

```
$rm one two three<CR>
$
```

Again Using **ls**, verify that there are three less files:

```
$ls<CR>
Part_1
Part_2
app_a
five
four
table
template
$
```

Like the **mv** command, **rm** requires caution. Once removed, a file can't be restored unless backups are kept on your system.

CHECK YOURSELF

1. Make a copy of your **.profile** file. Name the new file **one**.

2. List your files.

3. Copy **one** to **two**.

4. List your files.

5. Move **one** to **three**.

6. List your files.

7. Remove all three files.

8. List your files.

ANSWERS

1. Enter **cp .profile one**.

2. Use **ls**.

3. Enter **cp one two**.

4. Use **ls**.

5. Enter **mv one three**.

6. Use **ls**.

7. Enter **rm one two three**.

8. Use **ls**.

Viewing Files

There are several ways in which to examine the contents of one or more files without using the **vi** editor. The simplest command is **cat**, short for *concatenate*. To view a single file with **cat** just provide the filename as an argument. Figure 4.1 provides an example using a small file.

The file, **one,** only has a handful of lines, so it fits nicely on the screen. You can provide multiple filenames to the **cat** command, as illustrated in Figure 4.2, and they concatenate together and are presented on the screen. The original files remain intact.

Both file **one** and file **two** are extremely small, and, combined with the **cat** command, they're small enough to fit on a single screen. However, only the bottom portion of large files are visible, because earlier portions scroll off the screen to make room for additional lines. The **cat** command by itself isn't very useful in such a situation. However, as you'll see later, it has important uses elsewhere.

▼ *Figure 4.1. Terminal Screen after Issuing* cat one

$cat one<CR>

1. Introducing UNIX

Before learning how to use UNIX, this chapter
provides you with some background information
that may be of some interest to you. In this
chapter, the following topics are covered:
$

What's required for large files is a method for displaying a
page at a time on the screen. There are two UNIX commands that
accomplish this: **more** and **pg**. Both commands allow you to page

---

▼ *Figure 4.2. Terminal Screen after Issuing* cat one two

$cat one two<CR>

1. Introducing UNIX

Before learning how to use UNIX, this chapter
provides you with some background information
that may be of some interest to you. In this
chapter, the following topics are covered:

2. Getting Started

The first steps toward learning about UNIX are how to gain
access to the system, become familiar with your
new surroundings, and perform some simple tasks to
get a feel for the system.
In this chapter, you'll learn about:

$

---

forward through a file; **pg** provides the additional capability of paging backward. First, look at **more**. Figure 4.3 displays the screen after issuing the **more** command on several files.

After the command is issued, the screen fills with as many lines as possible from the specified file or files. The —**More**— message is on the last line, indicating that there's more to view, along with a message that indicates the percentage of the file or files viewed thus far. At this point you instruct the **more** command what to do next. The easiest step is simply to press the Spacebar (**SPACE**) key to view the next pageful (Figure 4.4).

Notice that the percentage of text displayed adjusted, and a new page of text comes into view. Again, **more** waits for you to tell it what to do next. You know how to advance to the next page, but

Viewing Files

▼ *Figure 4.3. Terminal Screen after Issuing* more one two

$more one two three<CR>

1. Introducing UNIX

Before learning how to use UNIX, this chapter
provides you with some background information
that may be of some interest to you. In this
chapter, the following topics are covered:

2. Getting Started

The first steps toward learning about UNIX are to gain
access to the system, become familiar with your
new surroundings, and perform some simple tasks to
get a feel for the system.
In this chapter, you'll learn about:

3. Editing Files with vi

This chapter allows you to work with some of
—**More**—**(10%)**

▼ *Figure 4.4. Terminal Screen after Pressing the Spacebar Key*

The basic features of the visual editor, **vi** (pronounced vee-eye), that you need in order to create and modify your own files, including cursor movement, inserting text, paging, searching, and text replacement. Additional features of **vi** covered later in Part II. In this chapter, you'll learn about:

      o Files and filenames
      o The vi editor
      o Editing modes
      o Editing a file
      o Inserting text
      o Cursor motion
      o Deleting text
      o Searching

In this chapter, the position of the cursor on the screen is represented by the square brackets, [ ], which surround a character. The position of the cursor is important in **vi**.
—More—(20%)

---

what else can you do with **more**? There are mechanisms for jumping forward blocks of lines, screens, even files; searching for patterns of text, invoking the **vi** editor, and more. Table 4.1 presents you with some of these actions.

For those commands listed in Table 4.1 where the **k** precedes the command, you may specify any integer number or just use the command with no number. In the latter case, appropriate default values will be used.

The other pagination command found on the UNIX system is **pg,** that a relatively new command might not be available on some of the older UNIX systems. **pg** is called up in the same manner as **more**—by listing the files to be displayed after the **pg** command:

```
$pg one two three<CR>
```

▼ *Table 4.1. Common—More—Prompt Requests for* more *Command*

Command	Resultant Action
h	Displays a description of all **more** commands
<CR>	Displays next line
<SPACE>	Displays next page
k/<search pattern>	Searches for *k*th occurrence of search pattern
q	Exits from more
d	Scrolls 11 lines down
ks	Skip forward *k* lines of text
kf	Skip forward *k* screenfuls of text
k:n	Skip forward *k* files
k:p	Skip backward *k* files
v	Starts **vi** on current file at current line
	Upon exiting **vi** will return to **more**

pg displays a slightly different screen than **more** (Figure 4.5).

Not only is the **pg** prompt different from the **more** prompt, but some of the **pg** commands are different from the **more** commands. Table 4.2 lists the **pg** commands.

There are also UNIX commands that enable you to view either the beginning or end of the file: They're called **head** and **tail**. In their simplest form, the commands are followed by the name of the file to be viewed. **head** displays the first ten lines of the file, while **tail** displays the last ten lines. Figures 4.6 and 4.7 illustrate the simplest ways of using these commands.

The **head** command allows you to specify the number of lines to be displayed. Type the command name, **head**, followed by a dash (-). Enter the number of lines you want to be displayed. Then type the filename. For example, Figure 4.8 requests that the first five lines of the file, **three**, be displayed.

The **tail** command offers several options, the most useful of which is the ability to specify how many lines from the bottom of the file to start displaying text. The default is set to ten. However, you can start anywhere in the file relative either to the top or bottom of the file. To do this, use either the plus (+) or minus (-) sign, followed by the number of lines. The plus offsets from the top of the file, while the minus offsets from the bottom of the file. For ex-

▼ *Figure 4.5.* **Terminal Screen after Issuing** *pg one two three*

1. Introducing UNIX

Before learning how to use UNIX, this chapter provides you with some background information that may be of some interest to you. In this chapter, the following topics are covered:

2. Getting Started

The first steps toward learning about UNIX are to gain access to the system, become familiar with your new surroundings, and perform some simple tasks to get a feel for the system. In this chapter, you'll learn about:

3. Editing Files with vi

This chapter allows you to work with some of

:

ample, **+25** means to begin display of the text 25 lines from the top of the file. A **-25** would mean to begin display 25 lines up from the bottom. Figure 4.9 uses an offset from the bottom of the file.

CHECK YOURSELF

Select a file that's larger than 24 lines.

1. Display the entire file on the screen.

2. Display one page at a time, moving forward.

3. Display one page at a time, moving both forward and backward in the file.

4. Display the first 12 lines of the file.

5. Display the last 12 lines of the file.

ANSWERS

1. Use either **cat** or **tail +1**.

2. Use either **more** or **pg**.

3. Use **pg**.

4. Use **head -12**.

5. Use **tail -12**.

▼ *Table 4.2. Common : Prompt Requests for* pg

Command	Resultant Action
h	Displays a description of all pg commands
<CR>	Displays next screenful of text
k/**<search pattern>/**	Searches for *k*th occurrence of search pattern
k?**<search pattern>?**	Searches backward for *k*th occurrence of search pattern
q	Exits from **pg**
+d	Scrolls half a screen forward (+ is optional)
-d	Scrolls half a screen backward
+*k*l	Skip forward *k* lines of text (+ is optional)
-*k*l	Skip backward *k* lines of text
+*k*f	Skip forward *k* screenfuls of text (+ is optional)
-*k*f	Skip backward *k* screenfuls of text
*k***n**	Skip forward *k* files
*k***p**	Skip backward *k* files

▼ *Figure 4.6. Terminal Screen after Issuing* head three

$head three\<CR>

3. Editing Files with vi

This chapter allows you to work with some of the basic features of the visual editor, **vi** (pronounced vee-eye), that you need in order to create and modify your own files, including cursor movement, inserting text, paging, searching, and text replacement. Additional features of **vi**
$

▼ *Figure 4.7. Terminal Screen after Issuing* tail three

$tail three\<CR>
Summary
In this chapter you've learned some of the elementary commands for managing your files on disk. However, their use has been limited thus far to your own personal disk storage area. You'll see more of these commands as you become more familiar with UNIX. In the next chapter you'll learn about the UNIX file system structure.
$

▼ *Figure 4.8. Terminal Screen after Issuing* head -5 three

$head -5 three\<CR>
3. Editing Files with vi
This chapter allows you to work with some of
$

▼ *Figure 4.9. **Terminal Screen after Issuing** tail -15 three*

$tail -15 three\<CR>
At some time in the future, you'll see a message on the terminal screen:

lp: printer request lp2-237 has been printer on printer lp2

Summary

In this chapter you've learned some of the elementary commands for managing your files on disk. However, their use has been limited thus far to your own personal disk storage area. You'll see more of these commands as you become more familiar with UNIX. In the next chapter you'll learn about the UNIX file system structure.
$

Printing Files

The basic UNIX command for printing is **lp**, which is short for *line printer*. In its simplest form, you can issue the command with a list of filenames as arguments. In this mode of operation, **lp** uses the default system printer for printing the file or files you specify:

```
$lp one<CR>
request id is lp1-234 (1 file)
$
```

Because many users usually share the printer, the system must identify individual print jobs. As in the example above, the system responds with a message that indicates the *lp request id* (lp1-234) for the particular print job. **lp1** designates the printer; **234** identifies the job number on that printer. The request id is especially important in a later chapter in which you learn how to manage print jobs.

If there are several printers on your system, you might want to specify one other than the default printer. Perhaps the default printer is a 132-column line printer, but you prefer to use an 80-column printer. The **lp** command allows you to override the default printer, but you need to know the name of the printer to which you want to send the job:

```
$lp -dlp2 one<CR>
request id is lp2-235 (1 file)
$
```

lp offers several other useful commands. For example, **lp** allows you to make multiple copies of the file or files that you send to it, using the **-n***i* option (*i* specifies the number of copies):

```
$lp -dlp2 -n2 one<CR>
request id is lp2-236 (1 file)
$
```

Another option, **-w**, instructs **lp** to write a message on your terminal when the print job is complete:

```
$lp -dlp2 -w one<CR>
request id is lp2-237 (1 file)
$
```

When the print job is complete, you see a message on the terminal screen:

```
lp: printer request lp2-237 has been printed on
printer lp2
```

QUICK SUMMARY

Command	Description
ls	list files
cp	copy files
mv	move files
rm	remove files
cat	concatenate files
more	page files
pg	page files
head	display top of file
tail	display bottom of file
lp	print files

PRACTICE WHAT YOU'VE LEARNED

These exercises provide practice working with files. Create a few practice files using **vi** before trying these exercises.

What You Should Do	How the Computer Responds
1. Use **ls** to list your files. Try using different options.	1. Displays a list of files.
2. Use **cp** to copy one of your files and name it **fun**. Use **ls** to list files.	2. Displays a list of files that includes **fun**.
3. Use **mv** to move **fun** to **new**. Use **ls** to list files.	3. Displays a list of files, that includes **new**.
4. Use **rm** to remove **new**. Use **ls** to list files.	4. Displays a list of files. **new** doesn't appear in the list.
5. Use **cat** to display several files.	5. Displays the contents of the files, one after another.
6. Use **more** to display the same set of files.	6. Displays the contents of the files, one page at a time. You have to instruct **more** to advance to each page.
7. Repeat step 6, but use **pg**.	7. Same results as step 6, but the prompt and commands differ from **pg**. Use **pg** to page back.
8. Select a file and use **lp** to print it (assuming there's a printer attached to your system).	8. Prints the file and displays a message indicating the lp request id..

WHAT IF IT DOESN'T WORK?

1. A number of the commands you use in this exercise might produce an error message indicating that a file can't be opened. The most likely cause of this error is mistyping the filename that you're asking the command to act upon.

2. If you receive the message, "files are identical," or, "a file cannot be copied to itself," then both filenames given to the **cp** or **mv** command are the same file.

3. If the commands produce error messages such as, "cannot create" or, "permission denied," there's something wrong with your personal storage area. See your system administrator.

UNIX File System

Files are a key element to the UNIX operating system. UNIX provides you with the capability to organize your files by using a special type of file called *a directory*. The entire UNIX system is organized into a hierarchy of directories and files called *the file system*. You have your own, private, file storage area, and so do other system users. UNIX facilitates the sharing of files, programs, devices, and other resources through the file system. To maximize your use of UNIX, it's important to understand how the file system is organized, how to navigate around it, and how to work with it. In this chapter, you'll learn about:

- ▲ Files and directories
- ▲ Creating, changing, and removing directories
- ▲ File system structure
- ▲ Where am I?
- ▲ Getting around
- ▲ Using pathnames with commands
- ▲ File permissions
- ▲ Owners and groups

Files and Directories

So far, you've learned how to create and modify regular files using the **vi** screen editor, and how to manipulate the files in your personal storage area, using UNIX commands such as **cp**, **mv**, **rm**, and so on.

Regular files are just one type of file taken from a larger class of files called *ordinary files*. Commands such as **who**, **vi**, and **date** are also stored in a type of ordinary file called an executable file. Another class of files that UNIX supports are called *directory files* or, simply, *directories*. A directory is a grouping mechanism that allows you to organize your files into categories or collections of files under a single name. Directories are often compared to the drawers of a file cabinet; files are often compared to the file folders contained within the cabinet drawers. But this analogy is too simple. Not only can directories contain ordinary files, but also other directories. This provides the user with a great deal of flexibility in building a personal directory structure.

There are UNIX commands that allow you to create, destroy, and move among directories. The next several sections introduce these commands to you and show you how to organize your files with directories.

Creating Directories

To create a directory, use the **mkdir** command, followed by the filename of the new directory. Perhaps you want to create a directory in which to store a file such as **phone**. A possible filename for such a directory is **Misc,** for Miscellaneous:

```
$mkdir Misc<CR>
$
```

A directory file named **Misc** has been created. To verify that this file exists, use the **ls** command:

```
$ls<CR>
Misc
phone
$
```

Notice that the name of the directory file begins with an upper-case letter. This is a convention, not a rule. However, following the convention makes it easier to distinguish directories from ordinary files when using **ls**. But don't depend upon the convention. To discover which files are directories, use the **-F** option with the **ls** command:

```
$ls -F<CR>
Misc/phone
$
```

Notice the slash (/) that appears after the filename **Misc**. It indicates that **Misc** is a directory, not an ordinary file.

Once you create a directory, there are a number of ways in which to work with it. For example, you can use **mv** to move the file, **phone**, into the new directory:

```
$mv phone Misc<CR>
$ls<CR>
Misc
$
```

The **phone** file is no longer listed by **ls** because you moved it to another directory, namely **Misc**. Why didn't the **mv** command use the second filename, **Misc**, as an ordinary file and overwrite it with the contents of **mv**? Because **mv** recognized that **Misc** was the name of a directory and therefore moved the file **phone** to that directory.

Changing Directories

UNIX has a feature called *the current directory*, which allows you to focus on a single directory at a time. With this feature, commands only operate on the current directory, unless directed otherwise. To change from the current directory, issue the **cd** (Change Directory) command, followed by the name of the directory to which you want to move. The following sequence of commands moves you to the **Misc** directory, and then shows you the **phone** file that was previously moved to that directory:

```
$ls -F<CR>
```

```
Misc/
$cd Misc<CR>
$ls -F<CR>
phone
$
```

Perhaps in the **Misc** directory you want to build an **Addresses** directory that contains addresses in individual files within that directory. While in the **Misc** directory, execute the following commands:

```
$mkdir Addresses<CR>
$ls -F<CR>
Addresses/
phone
$cd Addresses<CR>
$ls -F<CR>
$
```

The final **ls** command issued in the above example shows that there aren't yet any files in the **Addresses** directory.

What if you need to move in the upward direction back to the level above the **Misc** directory? By issuing the **cd** command with the special filename, .., you move to that level because every file or directory has only one parent directory. Otherwise, **cd ..** wouldn't know where to go! Starting in the **Addresses** directory for **gwl**, move back to your original starting point in two moves:

```
$cd ..<CR>
$ls -F<CR>
Addresses/
phone
$cd ..<CR>
$ls -F<CR>
Misc/
$
```

Not only can the .. special filename be used with **cd**, but with other commands as well. For example, you can also copy files into a directory using the **cp** command.

```
$ls -F<CR>
Misc/
```

```
$cd Misc<CR>
$ls -F<CR>
Addresses/
phone
$cp phone ..<CR>
$cd ..<CR>
$ls -F<CR>
Misc/
phone
$
```

Now two copies of the **phone** file exist in two different directories. Notice that each can use the same name. This is because names are unique to *each directory*.

Removing Directories

To remove a directory, use the **rmdir** command:

```
$ls -F<CR>
Misc/
phone
$rmdir Misc<CR>
rmdir: Misc not empty
$
```

Notice that the command to remove the directory, **Misc**, resulted in an error message! Why? Because UNIX doesn't allow you to use **rmdir** to remove a directory that has other files within it. So, you first must do something with the files in **Misc** before removing it.

```
$cd Misc<CR>
$ls -F<CR>
Addresses/
phone
$rmdir Addresses<CR>
$ls -F<CR>
phone
$rm phone<CR>
$cd ..<CR>

$ls<CR>
```

```
Misc
phone
$rmdir Misc
$ls<CR>
phone
$
```

UNIX provides a means to more simply remove a directory. Use the **rm** command along with the **-r** option. This option directs **rm** to remove all files contained in the list of files. If those directories contain other directories, then **rm** removes any files in those directories as well. In other words, if you want to get rid of the **Misc** directory, and all files and directories from that point on, you can do so with a single command.

```
$ls -F<CR>
Misc/
$rmdir Misc<CR>
rmdir: Misc not empty
$rm -r Misc<CR>
$ls -F<CR>
$
```

Now **Misc**, and everything below it (the **Addresses** directory and the **phone** file) are gone.

TIP

Be careful using rm -r. **If you accidentally include a directory that you don't want to remove, there's no way to prevent** rm **from removing it!**

Make sure to use the appropriate remove command for the specific type of file you wish to remove. For example, removing ordinary files with **rmdir,** or removing directories with **rm** (without the **-r** option), produces an error message:

```
$ls -F<CR>
Misc/
phone
$rm Misc<CR>
rm: Misc directory
$rmdir phone<CR>
```

```
rmdir: phone not a directory
$
```

CHECK YOURSELF

1. Create a directory called **Test**.

2. Change to this directory.

3. Create three new directories called **One**, **Two**, and **Three**. List them.

4. Change into each directory, create some files, and list them.

5. Change back to your original directory and remove all the files and directories you just created.

ANSWERS

1. Enter **mkdir Test**.

2. Enter **cd Test**.

3. Enter the commands: **mkdir One**, **mkdir Two**, **mkdir Three**, and **ls -F**.

4. For each of these directories perform the following steps: **cd** to the directories; use **vi** to create some files; use **ls -F**, and then **cd ...**.

5. Enter **cd ..** to get above the three directories; and then enter **rm - rTest**.

File System Structure

So far your view of UNIX has been limited to your own personal storage area where you're free to create and remove files and directories. However, there are probably other users on the same UNIX system as you. They have personal storage areas as well. Your personal storage area is actually a directory contained within a larger set of directories and files called *the UNIX file system*.

All resources available to you on UNIX are provided through the file system. All the commands are actually files, whose filename is the same as the command name. When you type a command name, it executes that file. These files reside in one of several standard directories within the file system. The shell knows which directories to look in when trying to locate a command in order to execute it. In addition, your login directory and those of other users on the system also are part of the file system. But how does it all fit together? And how can you make use of the file system? To answer these questions you'll learn about the organization of the file system, how to name mechanisms, and how to move around the file system.

The UNIX file system is hierarchical in nature and forms a tree structure. The beginning of the file system is called the *root directory* or *root*. The filename for this special directory is / (slash). Recall from Chapter 3 that the slash is the only character that you can't use in creating a filename. The remainder of the file system expands into an inverted tree from the root directory. For example, Figure 5.1 illustrates a selected subset of a UNIX file system.

In Figure 5.1 the circles represent directories, and the squares represent ordinary files. Notice that the **phone** example from Chapter 2 appears in the **gwl** directory. Also, some of the commands you learned in earlier chapters appear in the **bin** directory. Further notice that the **gwl** directory is contained within the **users** directory, which in turn is contained within the root (/) directory. All ordinary files are found within a directory and all directories, except the root

▼ *Figure 5.1. UNIX File System*

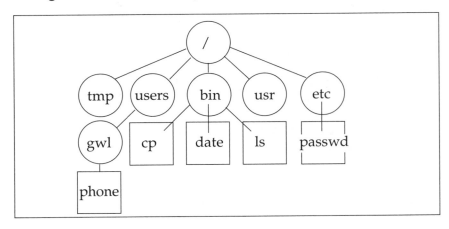

directory, are contained within other directories. Directories may contain a combination of ordinary files and other directories.

Where Am I?

When you login, you're positioned in what's called your *home directory*. This is the directory in which your personal files are stored. There's an environment variable, **$HOME**, which is set when you login. To find out where your home directory is located, simply type:

```
$echo $HOME<CR>
/users/gwl
$
```

Compare the output of the **echo $HOME** command with the layout of the file system in Figure 5.1. Notice that starting with **root** (/), each directory down the tree is named to form a path to the home directory, **gwl**. The slash is also used to separate filenames within a *full pathname*. The slash (/) between the **users** and **gwl** directories serves this purpose.

You can also find out where your home directory is by using the **pwd** command, short for *Print Working Directory*:

```
$pwd<CR>
/users/gwl
$
```

The Print Working Directory refers to the directory in which you're currently located within the file system. This reference helps you move around the file system.

Getting Around

To change to a different directory, just issue the **cd** command, followed by the name of the directory to which you want to move. There are two different ways in which to specify a directory. The first way is called an *absolute path*. An absolute path specifies a path to a directory, starting from the root of the file system. These types of pathnames always begin with a slash (/). For example, if you want to see what's in the **bin** directory, simply use the following command line:

```
$cd /bin<CR>
$ls<CR>
cp
cat
date
echo
ps
rmdir
who
$
```

Note: There are actually many more commands stored in the **/bin** directory, but only a select few are shown above.

Use the **pwd** command to verify that the **cd** command actually made the move that you expect:

```
$pwd<CR>
/bin
$
```

Another method of changing directories is by using *relative pathnames*. Rather than using the root directory (/) as the starting point to form an absolute pathname, use the current working directory. Hence, the pathname you use is *relative* to the current directory. As long as you're moving to a directory below the current directory, all you have to do is enter a series of names separated by slashes (/) to form a path from here to there. For example, move to the root directory (/) using **cd**:

```
$cd /<CR>
$pwd<CR>
/
$
```

Now, you're positioned in the root directory and can move into any directory below it. There are a number of ways to get back to your home directory. For example, you can use **cd** to move into the **users** directory:

```
$cd users<CR>
$pwd<CR>
/users
$
```

Notice that the filename **users** isn't preceded by a slash (/) when using the **cd** command. This causes **cd** to look for a directory named **users** in the current directory, and to change to that directory. If there's no directory named **users** in the current directory, then an error message appears:

```
$cd users<CR>
users: bad directory
$
```

However, in this example, the directory does exist. Complete the move by issuing another **cd** command to move into the **gwl** directory:

```
$cd gwl<CR>
$pwd<CR>
/users/gwl
$
```

The same move can be accomplished by issuing a single **cd** command. First, change (**cd**) back to the root directory, and then jump to **gwl** in a single move:

```
$pwd<CR>
/users/gwl
$cd /<CR>
$pwd<CR>
/
$cd users/gwl<CR>
$pwd<CR>
/users/gwl
$
```

This technique works if you're moving down the tree from your current position. If you want to move up the tree toward the root directory, issue the **cd** command with the special filename, **..** . Starting from the home directory for **gwl**, the current directory changes to the root directory in two moves:

```
$pwd<CR>
/users/gwl
$cd ..<CR>
$pwd<CR>
/users
```

```
$cd ..<CR>
$pwd<CR>
/
$
```

This change can also be made in a single step:

```
$pwd<CR>
/users/gwl
$cd ../..<CR>
$pwd<CR>
/
$
```

The **cd** command can also be issued without specifying a directory. This way, **cd** defaults to your home directory. So, to go back to your home directory, simply type **cd**, or **cd $HOME**.

CHECK YOURSELF

1. Starting in your home directory, move up one level, and find out where you are located.

2. Change to the **/usr** directory and find out where you are located.

3. Change to the **/usr/bin** directory and find out where you are located.

4. Change to the **/usr/lib** directory and find out where you are located.

5. Change to your home directory and find out where you are located.

ANSWERS

1. Enter the **cd ..** command, followed by **pwd**.

2. Enter the **cd /usr** command, followed by **pwd**.

3. Enter the **cd /bin** command, followed by **pwd**.

4. Enter the **cd ../lib** command, followed by **pwd**.

5. Enter the **cd** command, followed by **pwd**.

Using Pathnames with Commands

When using the **ls** command, you're limited to listing the contents of the current directory. To examine the contents of another directory, use **cd** to change the current directory; then issue the **ls** command, or provide the **ls** command with the pathname to the directory for which you want a listing. For example, to see what's in the directory **/usr**:

```
$ls /usr<CR>
adm
bin
games
include
lib
local
lost+found
mail
man
preserve
pub
spool
tmp
$
```

Any command that accepts filenames as arguments also accepts full pathnames as well. For example, you can copy files that are in your own HOME directory, as well as those that are in directories for which you have authorization. For instance, if your friend **brad** has a login on your system, and his login is also in the **users** directory, you can copy his files into your directory (if you're authorized). If **brad** has a file named **phone**, copy his file, **phone**, and provide the copy with a different name:

```
$cp ../brad/phone new_phone<CR>
$
```

File Permissions

UNIX provides a security mechanism that enables you to specify permission levels upon your directories and files. This mechanism lets you control access to your files. Before learning how to specify permissions, you'll learn what they are and how they work.

With *read permission*, you can look at a file using **cat, more, vi**, and other commands; and you can copy (**cp**) or print (**lp**) files. With *write permission*, you can move (**mv**), remove (**rm**), or change (**vi**) a file. With *execute permission*, you can declare that a file is an executable command (to be discussed in a later chapter).

For directory files, the three permission levels take on different meanings. To list (**ls**) the contents of a directory, you must have read permission. To change directory (**cd**), you must have both read and execute permissions. (For directories, the execute permission actually means search permission.) To create files in a directory, you must have write permission. To edit or remove a file, you must have write permission on both the file you wish to work with and the directory in which the file is contained.

For any given file or directory, there exist three possible *levels of access*: the owner of the file or directory, logins that belong to the same group as the owner of the file or directory, and everyone else on the system. Separate sets of read, write, and execute permissions can be set for each of these three categories.

All logins belong to at least one group, and possibly more. Groups are put together by the system administrator. Groups allow you to set up permissions on your files and directories for members of your group, yet protect files and directories from others on the system who don't belong to your group. Files and directories also belong to groups. When you create a file or directory, the group is automatically determined based upon the group your login belongs to.

TIP

Older versions of UNIX derived from System V, such as Xenix, only allow a login to belong to a single group. Versions of UNIX derived from Berkeley UNIX, such as SunOS, allow logins to belong to multiple groups. System V Release 4 allows multiple group membership.

There's an option that you can provide to the **ls** command that allows you to examine the permissions on files and directories. It's the **-l** option, which directs **ls** to provide you with a long listing.

```
$ls -l<CR>
total 4
drwxr-xr-x  2 gwl  devel  32   Feb 24 09:46 Addresses
-rw-r---    1 gwl  devel  6    Jan 12 19:28 phone
$
```

When used with no filename arguments, this option first provides you with the total number of *disk blocks* used by the current directory (total 4 in this case). The lines that follow specify the *permission modes, number of links, owner, group, number of bytes or characters, modification date and time,* and *filename.* The important information to focus upon at the moment is the leading set of ten characters starting in column 1:

```
drwxr-xr-x  2 gwl  devel  32   Feb 24 09:46 Addresses
-rw-r---    1 gwl  devel  6    Jan 12 19:28 phone
```

The first character designates the type of file. **d** designates directory and the **-** designates an ordinary file. The remaining nine characters specify three levels of permissions. The first three characters specify the permissions for the owner of the files, **gwl** in this example:

```
drwxr-xr-x  2 gwl  devel  32   Feb 24 09:46 Addresses
-rw-r---    1 gwl  devel  6    Jan 12 19:28 phone
```

The next three characters specify permissions for the group, **devel** in this case:

```
drwxr-xr-x  2 gwl  devel  32   Feb 24 09:46 Addresses
-rw-r---    1 gwl  devel  6    Jan 12 19:28 phone
```

And the final three characters specify permissions for everyone else on the system, that is, users who don't belong to the group, **devel**:

```
drwxr-xr-x  2 gwl  devel  32   Feb 24 09:46 Addresses
-rw-r---    1 gwl  devel  6    Jan 12 19:28 phone
```

For each level of permission, the three characters are in a specific order, and have a specific meaning. For example, notice that what follows the initial **d** for the **Addresses** directory are the characters **rwx**. These characters indicate that the owner of the file has permission to read, **r**, write, **w**, and execute, **x**. The next three characters, **r-x,** indicate that members of the **devel** group have permission to read and search in that directory, but don't have permission to write in that directory. The **-** in the second position, between the three characters, indicates that the write permission has been turned off. The final three characters for **Addresses** indicate permission for everyone else on the system.

For the file, **phone**, the owner is allowed to read and write to the file, but not execute it (**rw-**). The members of the **devel** group are allowed to read the file, but are not allowed to write to it or execute it (**r—**). And users who aren't members of the **devel** group aren't allowed to do anything with the file (**—-**).

Now that you're familiar with file permissions and their purpose, you'll learn how to set them. Even though you've created files using **vi** and various other commands, you've not yet set permissions. Every file is created with a default set of permissions. By default, all directories are created with the permissions, **rwxr-xr-x.** And all ordinary files are created with the permissions, **rw-r—r—**. Execute permission must explicitly be requested, but you'll learn about this capability later.

To change the permission modes on a file, use the **chmod** command. There are two methods for specifying which permissions to change and how to change them. To keep it simple, you'll learn the method that's easier to remember. You use **chmod** with an option that's composed of three different parts, and follow the command with the list of files, separated by blanks. The three parts of the option specify: the level of permissions to change (**u** for file owner, **g** for group, **o** for others, **a** for all), the type of change (**+** to add, **-** to remove, **=** to set), and the permission modes to change (**r** for read, **w** for write, **x** for execute).

To make the **phone** file available for anyone to read, enter the **chmod** command as follows:

```
$ls -l phone<CR>
-rw-r—- 1 gwl devel 6 Jan 12 19:28 phone
$chmod o+r phone<CR>
```

```
$ls -l phone<CR>
-rw-r—r— 1 gwl devel 6 Jan 12 19:28 phone
$
```

The key aspect of the **chmod** command line is the **o+r** option. The three parts of this option indicate: for whom to change the permissions (**o** indicates others), how to change the permissions (**+** indicates to add to the existing set of permissions), and which permission modes to change (**r** indicates read). This option works very much like a mathematical expression. There are two operands (who and permission mode) and a single operator (**+**, **-**, or **=**).

To set all the permission modes in the **phone** file to include all three classes of users, issue the = operator. Using this operator destroys previous permission settings, unlike the + and - operators, which add or subtract permissions relative to the current settings:

```
$ls -l phone<CR>
-rw-r—— 1 gwl devel 6 Jan 12 19:28 phone
$chmod ugo=r phone<CR>
$ls -l phone<CR>
-r—r—r— 1 gwl devel 6 Jan 12 19:28 phone
$
```

Of course, now no user, not even you, can write to the file!

TIP

Even if there are no write permission modes set for a file, the owner can always remove a file. When the rm command is used on a file that has write permissions turned off, a message appears in the form of a question that asks the user to make a decision as to whether or not to remove the file. Enter a "y" for yes, or an "n" for no.

To correct the situation, add write permission for yourself:

```
$ls -l phone<CR>
-r—r—r— 1 gwl devel 6 Jan 12 19:28 phone
$chmod u+w phone<CR>
$ls -l phone<CR>
-rw-r—r— 1 gwl devel 6 Jan 12 19:28 phone
$
```

CHECK YOURSELF

1. Examine the permission modes of files in your home directory.

2. Select one file and protect it from all users, including yourself. Don't allow any access to the file.

3. Try to access this file using any UNIX command that operates upon files.

4. Now set permissions on this file to allow yourself read-only access.

5. Try to use the **vi** editor upon the file.

6. Try to move the file to a new name.

7. Add the write permission mode for the user of the file, which now has a new name from the previous move.

ANSWERS

1. Enter the **ls -l** command.

2. Use the **chmod a=** command upon one of the files. Enter the **ls -l** command to verify that all permissions are turned off for this file.

3. Use any of the folling commands upon the file: **vi, cp, mv, rm, cat, more,** and so on.

4. Use the **chmod u+r** command upon the file. Enter the **ls -l** command to verify that the read permission is set for the user of this file.

5. Notice that there's a [read only] message at the bottom of the **vi** screen. This means that you can't save any changes. Try it, then quit from **vi** using the **:q!**.

6. Use **mv** to move the file to a new name. Notice that you can do this. Why? Because permissions only impact the file, not the directory in which the file resides. Moving a file involves changing a directory entry, not the file itself!

7. Use the **chmod u+w** command upon the file's new name. Enter the **ls -l** command to verify that the write permission is set for the user of this file.

Owners and Groups

In addition to changing access permissions upon files or directories, the owner of a file or directory can change ownership or group membership of the file. Why is this necessary? Recall an earlier example:

```
$cp ../brad/phone new_phone<CR>
$
```

If you have permission to read both the directory, **../brad,** and the file, **../brad/phone**, then the file **../brad/phone** is copied to your directory under the name **new_phone**. You now own the copy of that file. However, if you want to move the file from **brad**'s directory to yours, don't forget that the owner of that file is still **brad**, not you. And, if you and **brad** belong to different groups, then the group id for the file is different as well. Using **ls -l** you can see this:

```
$mv ../brad/phone new_phone<CR>
$ls -l new_phone<CR>
-rw-rw-r— 1 brad devel 79 Feb 28 10:16 new_phone
$
```

If you have read, write, and execute permission for **brad**'s directory, and read and write permission for the file, the move works. However, the moved file is still owned by **brad**. This means that you must follow the permissions set for the group, even though the file currently resides in your directory. To change this situation, the current owner of the file, **brad**, must issue the **chown** command to change the owner of the file, and if needed, the **chgrp** command to change the group of the file. Until **brad** does this, you don't own the file. If **brad** issues the **chown** command *before* the **chgrp** command, then he won't be allowed to change the group because he's no longer the owner! You'll have to do it.

TIP

Even if you don't own a file in your directory, you can still delete it despite the fact that you may not have write permission to do so. This is because you own the directory: When you perform a remove (rm), you actually remove a directory entry for the file. This makes sense, otherwise someone might be able to deposit files in your directory that you don't want and you wouldn't be able to do anything about it.

To change the owner of a file using **chown**, the current owner of the file must supply the name of the file to change and the login of the new owner of the file. The user **brad** issues the following series of commands:

```
$cd ../gwl<CR>
$ls -l<CR>
total 6
drwxr-xr-x  2 gwl    devel   32 Feb 24 09:46 Addresses
-rw-rw-r—   1 brad   devel   79 Feb 28 10:16 new_phone
-rw-r—r—    1 gwl    devel    6 Jan 12 19:28 phone
$chown gwl new_phone<CR>
$ls -l<CR>
drwxr-xr-x  2 gwl    devel   32 Feb 24 09:46 Addresses
total 6
-rw-rw-r—   1 gwl    devel   79 Feb 28 10:16 new_phone
-rw-r—r—    1 gwl    devel    6 Jan 12 19:28 phone
$
```

If **brad** belongs to a group other than the **devel** group, then change the group of the file:

```
$ls -l<CR>
total 6
drwxr-xr-x  2 gwl    devel   32 Feb 24 09:46 Addresses
-rw-rw-r—   1 gwl    sales   79 Feb 28 10:16 new_phone
-rw-r—r—    1 gwl    devel    6 Jan 12 19:28 phone
$chgrp devel new_phone<CR>
new_phone: Not owner
$
```

Now that **brad** has issued the **chown** command, he no longer has permission to change the group of the file! You must do it. Alternatively, first change the group, and then the owner of the file to avoid this problem. Remember: To change owner or group, you must be the owner of the file. Immediately after issuing the **chown** command, ownership of a file is relinquished.

File System Structure

QUICK SUMMARY

Command	Description
mkdir	make a directory
cd	change directory
rmdir	remove directory
$HOME	shell environment variable that contains your home directory
pwd	print working directory
chmod	change mode
chown	change owner
chgrp	change group

PRACTICE WHAT YOU'VE LEARNED

These exercises give you practice working with the UNIX file system:

What You Should Do

1. Use **mkdir** to create a temporary directory called **Temp**. Use **ls** to list files.

2. Use **cd** to change directory to **Temp**. Use **pwd** to make sure it works.

3. Use **mkdir** to create another directory called **Test**. Use **ls** to list files.

4. Use **cd** to change directory to **Test**. Use **pwd** to make sure it works.

How the Computer Responds

1. Displays a list of files, including **Temp**.

2. Displays the full pathname to the **Temp** directory.

3. Displays a list of files, which consists only of **Test**.

4. Displays the full pathname to the **Test** directory.

What You Should Do	*How the Computer Responds*
5. Use **cp** to copy the /etc/**passwd** file to the current directory. Use **ls-l** to list files.	5. Displays a list of files, which consists only of **passwd**. Notice that the permissions on the file are read-only for owner, group, and everyone.
6. Use **chmod** to change the file permissions on **passwd** so that you're allowed to write to it. Use **ls-l** to list the files.	6. Displays the list of files. **passwd** now has write permission for you.
7. Use **mv** and a relative path name to move **passwd** up one level. Use **ls** to list files.	7. No files are listed by **ls**.
8. Use **cd** to change directory up one level and use **ls** to list files.	8. Displays a list of files, which consists of **Test** and **passwd**.
9. Use **pwd** to find out where you're located.	9. Displays the full pathname to the **Temp** directory.
10. Use **cd** to change directory to your home directory. Use **pwd** to find out where you're located.	10. Displays the full pathname to your home directory.
11. Use **rmdir** to remove the **Temp** directory.	11. The system indicates that the directory is not empty.
12. Use **rm -r Temp** to remove the Temp directory and all its decendents. Use **ls** to list files.	12. The **Temp** directory doesn't appear in the listing.

WHAT IF IT DOESN'T WORK?

1. If any execution of the **mkdir** command results in an error message indicating that it can't access the directory named in the command, then you're not allowed to create a directory. Use **pwd** to make sure you're in your home directory. If you

are, use **ls -l ..** | **more** to check the permissions on the parent directory where you're trying to create a new directory. If your home directory isn't owned by you, see your system administrator. If your home directory or any subdirectory below your home directory doesn't have write permission for you, use **chmod** to correct it.

2. If **cd** results in a "bad directory" message, make sure that you typed in the directory name correctly. If you did, do an **ls -l** to make sure the directory exists, and that you have permission to access it. In order to **cd** into a directory, you must have execute permission.

3. If **ls** results in a "bad directory" message, make sure that you have read permission on the directory you're currently in. You can **cd** into a directory, yet not be able to list any files in the directory if the read permission isn't set.

4. If the **cp /etc/passwd** command results in a "cannot open" or "permission denied" message, then first check the permissions on the file with **ls -l /etc/passwd**. You must have read permission on the file, and read and execute permission on the /**etc** directory. If this isn't the problem, check the directory you're currently in. Either the permissions on the directory don't allow you to write there, or there's a file by the same name in the directory that you're not allowed to overwrite. The same problems can occur with **mv**.

5. If either the **chmod** or **rm** commands produce error messages indicating that you can't change or remove the file, then you're not the owner of the file. Use **ls** to figure who is.

6

Putting
It All
Together

UNIX provides you with the ability to assemble various commands so that the output of one command may be fed into another. You may chain a number of commands together in this manner. This allows you to build powerful command lines from standard components much like an assembly line. The UNIX shell provides the glue that enables you to connect commands together using several mechanisms. In this chapter, you'll learn about:

▲ **I/O redirection**

▲ **Pipes**

▲ **Simple filters**

▲ **Shell metacharacters**

I/O Redirection

When a UNIX command runs, the output of the command is directed to the terminal screen. However, you might want to save the output of a command and store it in a file. UNIX provides an *output redirection* capability that allows you to send the output of a command to a file rather than to the terminal screen. To accomplish this, simply type a command with a > followed by a filename. The example below uses this mechanism to create a new file:

```
$echo hello, there > hello<CR>
$cat hello<CR>
hello, there
$
```

Redirection has some practical applications as well. The results of the **ls** command can be stored in a file as follows:

```
$ls -l > list<CR>
$
```

The snapshot provided by the **ls** command has been captured in the file, **list**, and can be examined with **cat**:

```
$cat list<CR>
total 6
drwxr-xr-x   2 gwl     devel    32 Feb 24 09:46 Addresses
-rw-r—r—     1 gwl     sales    79 Feb 28 10:16 new_phone
-rw-r—r—     1 gwl     devel     6 Jan 12 19:28 phone
$
```

Be careful when using the output redirection capability (>). If you're redirecting the output of a command to an existing file, its current contents will be overwritten and lost. For example, the information from the previous command contained in the **list** file will be lost if the following command line is executed:

```
$date > list<CR>
$cat list<CR>
Sun Mar 1 12:06:18 EST 1992
$
```

UNIX provides another output redirection option that allows you to append the output to a file rather than overwrite the current contents of the file. Instead of a single redirection symbol (**>**), use two (**>>**):

```
$date > list<CR>
$cat list<CR>
Sun Mar 1 12:06:18 EST 1992
$ls -l >> list<CR>
$cat list<CR>
Sun Mar 1 12:06:18 EST 1992
total 6
drwxr-xr-x  2 gwl    devel   32 Feb 24 09:46 Addresses
-rw-r—r—    1 gwl    sales   79 Feb 28 10:16 new_phone
-rw-r—r—    1 gwl    devel    6 Jan 12 19:28 phone
$
```

Notice that the result of the **date** command line is not lost. The output of the **ls** command was appended to the bottom of the file.

Once you've captured the output of a command in a file, you are able to use it as any other file. You can use the **vi** editor on it, copy it to another filename, print it, and so on.

Input can also be redirected from a file to a command. The symbol used for input redirection is **<**. Many of the commands you've seen thus far work with filenames as arguments. However, these commands also work with input that's been redirected from a file. For example:

```
$cat < list<CR>
Sun Mar 1 12:06:18 EST 1992
total 6
drwxr-xr-x  2 gwl    devel   32 Feb 24 09:46 Addresses
-rw-r—r—    1 gwl    sales   79 Feb 28 10:16 new_phone
-rw-r—r—    1 gwl    devel    6 Jan 12 19:28 phone
$
```

The **cat** command normally works with a list of files as arguments. However, when the input redirection symbol, **<**, is encountered, the **cat** command doesn't look for a list of files on the command line, but takes its input from the file that's being redirected to it.

There's no reason to use input redirection from a file with **cat** when you can just list the files on the command line. However, there are some UNIX commands that typically accept input interactively from the keyboard. For these types of commands, you can redirect the input to come from a file rather than the keyboard. For example, recall that the **bc** command allows you to perform calculations interactively. You can also prepare a file with the desired calculations and redirect input from that file to the command:

```
$cat numbers<CR>
3/2
5.4+3/4
2+4.3*3
$bc -l < numbers<CR>
1.50000000000000000000
6.15000000000000000000
14.9
$
```

If you want to store the results of the above command in a file rather than display them on the screen, you can. Both input and output redirection can be included on the same command line. For example:

```
$cat numbers<CR>
3/2
5.4+3/4
2+4.3*3
$bc -l < numbers > out<CR>
$cat out<CR>
1.50000000000000000000
6.15000000000000000000
14.9
$
```

The order in which the input and output redirection directives appear in the command line makes no difference to the shell. The following command line produces the same results:

```
$bc -l > out < numbers<CR>
$
```

However, using a filename on the left-hand side of the output redirection operator results in an error message:

```
$numbers > bc -l<CR>
numbers: execute permission denied
$
```

The error message indicates that the left-hand side of the output redirection operator doesn't constitute an executable program.

WARNING

Making the mistake of redirecting output instead of input can be dangerous.

```
$bc -l > numbers<CR>
$
```

Instead of redirecting input from the file, **numbers**, to the **bc** command, the **bc** command redirects the output to **numbers**. In the process, the original contents of **numbers** is overwritten!

CHECK YOURSELF

1. Save a list of the files in your current directory in a file named **new**.

2. View this new file with **more**.

3. Find out who is on the system and append the results to the **new** file.

ANSWERS

1. Use the **ls -l** command and redirect the output to a file named **new**.

2. Redirect input to the **more** command from the **new** file.

3. Execute the **who** command and redirect the output to append to the **new** file.

Pipes

The redirection of input and output is the simplest mechanism that UNIX provides for assembling components, files and commands, and typically takes place either at the beginning or end of a command line. In between, multiple commands can link together to form an assembly line in which the output of one command is passed to the next command as input, using a mechanism called *pipes*.

The reason that the input and output of a command may be redirected is because UNIX provides standard input and output interfaces, more commonly called *standard in and out. Standard input* is taken from the keyboard and *standard output* is put on the terminal. The redirection symbols alert the shell to modify this behavior, and UNIX allows the standard output of one command to become the standard input of another. The pipe is used to connect two commands in this manner. The symbol for a pipe on a UNIX command line is |. By inserting a pipe symbol, |, between two commands on a command line, the shell automatically performs the necessary work to link the two commands.

Earlier you learned about the **more** command. You can use the standard output of any UNIX command, along with a pipe symbol (|), to provide **more** with input:

```
$ls -l | more<CR>
```

The output of the **ls -l** command is displayed on the screen using **more** (Figure 6.1).

In this case, had the **ls -l** command been run without piping the output to the **more** command, the output would have scrolled right off the screen and only the last portion of the output would have been visible to you. By piping the output of **ls -l** to **more** you control the visibility of the output on the screen.

lp is another command that is often the recipient of piped input. You've seen **lp** work with files, but here's how it's used with a pipe:

```
$ls -l | lp<CR>
request id is lp1-240 (standard input)
$
```

▼ *Figure 6.1. Terminal Screen after Issuing ls -l | more*

```
$ls -l | more<CR>
total 242
-rw-r—r—      1 gwl    devel      216 Jan  7 13:41 App
-rw-rw-rw—    1 gwl    devel      464 Dec 29 22:13 Part_1
-rw-r—r—      1 gwl    devel      245 Jan  7 13:40 Part_2
-rw-r—r—      1 gwl    devel       29 Mar  1 12:06 a
-rw-r—r—      1 gwl    devel      242 Jan  1 14:30 app_a
-rw-r—r—      1 gwl    devel      603 Jan  1 14:30 app_b
-rw-r—r—      1 gwl    devel     1127 Jan  1 14:30 app_c
-rw-r—r—      1 gwl    devel     2356 Jan 16 21:36 app_e
-rw-r—r—      1 gwl    devel      974 Jan  1 14:31 app_f
-rw-r—r—      1 gwl    devel     1264 Jan 16 21:36 app_g
-rw-r—r—      1 gwl    devel        0 Mar  1 12:42 b
-rw-r—r—      1 gwl    devel      785 Jan  3 12:30 bill
-rw-r—r—      1 gwl    devel      732 Feb 28 08:16 check
-rw-r—r—      1 gwl    devel    31164 Mar  1 11:59 five
-rw-r—r—      1 gwl    devel     9986 Feb 26 09:50 four
-rw-r—r—      1 gwl    devel      821 Feb 24 19:54 l_bio
-rw-r—r—      1 gwl    devel     1443 Jan 16 21:36 letter
-rw-r—r—      1 gwl    devel     5042 Feb 26 11:31 one
-rw-r—r—      1 gwl    devel     1543 Jan 16 21:37 one.tmp
-rw-r—r—      1 gwl    devel     2008 Jan  6 19:16 people
-rw-r—r—      1 gwl    devel     1165 Jan  6 19:17 people_pic
—More—(65%)
```

Notice that the message that comes back from the **lp** command doesn't indicate the number of files, but instead indicates that the standard input is the source for the input to be printed.

There's also a command that formats the contents of files into pages with page numbers and headings. It's called **pr** and is very helpful when formatting the output of long files for printing. But to use it along with the **lp** command calls for a pipe:

```
$pr phone | lp<CR>
request id is lp1-241 (standard input)
$
```

The output from **pr** that appears on the printer breaks a file into pages and provides page numbering and a heading as follows:

```
Mar 6 08:25 1992 phone Page 1
Bradley G. Futia     813-555-5555
Monica L. Leach      813-555-5555
Marion Leach         908-555-5555
Cynthia Topfer       212-555-5555
Vincent Futia        201-555-5555
```

In this example, only one page is necessary. The **pr** command provides enough blank lines to fill one page of output (typically 66 lines). If there's enough information in the **phone** file, additional pages are generated with top and bottom margins and page numbers.

To send the output to the terminal screen using **pr**, you need to adjust the number of lines per page to suit a terminal screen's capacity. **pr** can be issued with the **-l** (lowercase **L**) option followed by the number of lines per page you wish. When combined with the **more** command by a pipe, you can format and control the output on the screen:

```
$pr -l24 phone | more<CR>
Mar 6 08:25 1992 phone Page 1
Bradley G. Futia     813-555-5555
Monica L. Leach      813-555-5555
Marion Leach         908-555-5555
Cynthia Topfer       212-555-5555
Vincent Futia        201-555-5555
$
```

You can combine input redirection and pipes within a single command line. For example, the following command line redirects input from the **numbers** file to the **bc** command, and then sends the output to the **more** command via a pipe.

```
$bc -l < numbers | more<CR>
1.50000000000000000000
6.15000000000000000000
14.9
$
```

The combination of i/o redirection and pipes is a powerful mechanism for putting together small programs dynamically in order to perform ad hoc tasks. UNIX also provides a number of utility programs to aid in building such combinations, which you'll see in later chapters.

Simple Filters

When one or more commands are connected by pipes, you have a *pipeline*. So far, you've only used pipes to convert the output of one command into the input of another. However, UNIX provides utility programs that may be inserted between the originating and terminating programs on a pipeline. These programs take input from standard input, transform the information in some form, and then output the results to standard output for further processing. These types of utilities are called *filters*.

For example, the **pr** command can be inserted into a pipeline as a filter program. It accepts input from standard input, which is connected to the output of another program by a pipe, and sends its output to standard output, which is connected to yet another pipe:

```
$ls -l | pr | lp<CR>
request id is lp1-242 (standard input)
$
```

The output of the **ls -l** command is sent to the **pr** command via the first pipe. The output of the **pr** command is then sent to the **lp** command through the second pipe. The data is sent down the pipeline much as water passes through a series of pipes, through a filtration system, to your sink.

Another very simple filter is called **sort**. **sort** is a UNIX command that can act upon one or more files provided as arguments. However, it can also act upon standard input. The output of the command is placed on the standard output. For example, recall the **phone** file from an earlier chapter:

```
$cat phone<CR>
Bradley G. Futia     813-555-5555
Monica L. Leach      813-555-5555
Marion Leach         908-555-5555
```

```
$ls *phone<CR>
new_phone
phone
$
```

This time, the pattern to be matched by the shell is any file whose filename ends with the characters **phone**.

The asterisk provides you with the capability to perform commands upon a number of files with relatively few keystrokes. The following command line allows you to edit each file in the current directory using **vi**:

```
$vi *<CR>
```

When you're done editing one file, the shell starts **vi** on the next one.

The following command line produces a list of files, all of which have double e's in their filename.

```
$ls *ee*<CR>
three
tree.pic
$
```

The asterisk (*) metacharacter can also be inserted between a series of characters:

```
$ls t*r*<CR>
three
trademarks
train
tree.pic
$
```

The match includes any number of characters, even none! This explains the reason for which the last three filenames, **trademarks, train**, and **tree.pic** are included. There are no characters between the **t** and **r** that matched the search criteria.

Another useful pattern-matching metacharacter is the question mark, **?**. When used in a command, the question means, "match any single character." If you enter **???**, UNIX matches three character filenames, as in the following example:

```
$ls ???<CR>
App
```

```
one
six
tip
two
$
```

You can also combine different metacharacters to form a single pattern-matching specification:

```
$ls ????*<CR>
Part_1
Part_2
five
four
people
people_pic
table
three
trademarks
train
tree.pic
$
```

The four question marks indicate that there must be four characters in a filename. The trailing asterisk indicates that there could be zero or more characters that follow. So this specification picks up all filenames with at least four characters in the name.

Another possible use is:

```
$ls t?ee*<CR>
tree.pic
$
```

The question mark matches one and only one character between the **t** and **ee**. That is why **tree.pic** matches but **three** doesn't.

QUICK SUMMARY

Command	Description
>	output redirection symbol
>>	output redirection append symbol
<	input redirection symbol
		pipe symbol

Command	Description
pr	file formatter
sort	sort utility
*	shell metacharacter matches any number of characters
?	shell metacharacter matches one character

PRACTICE WHAT YOU'VE LEARNED

The following exercises combine the commands you learned in earlier chapters with i/o redirection, pipes, shell metacharacters, and filters.

What You Should Do

1. Use the **sort** command to sort the **/etc/passwd** file and pipe the output to the **lp** command.

2. Use **ls -l** to list the contents of the **/bin** directory and pipe the output to the **more** command to view it on the screen.

3. Use **who** to find out who is on the system and redirect the output to a file called **who_now**.

4. Use **pr-124** to format the file **who_now** and pipe the output to the **more** command.

5. Use the **pr** command to format the same file for output on a printer, and pipe the output to the **lp** command.

6. List all the commands in the **/bin** directory that start with the letter "**c**."

How the Computer Responds

1. Displays a message indicating the lp request id and outputs the sorted version of **/etc/passwd** to the printer.

2. Displays the initial 24 lines of output. Use the **more** command to page through the output.

3. Displays the UNIX prompt. A new file called **who_now** is created in the current directory.

4. Displays formatted version of the file. Use the **more** command to advance to a new page.

5. Displays a message indicating the lp request id and outputs the formatted version of **who_now** to the printer.

6. Displays the list on the screen.

What You Should Do	**How the Computer Responds**
7. List all the commands in the **/bin** directory that start with the letter "**c**" and contain only two characters in the name.	7. Displays the list on the screen.
8. Use the **date** command and redirect the output to a file called **todays_date**.	8. Displays the UNIX prompt. A new file called **todays_date** is created in the current directory.
9. Use the **cal** command to obtain this month's calendar and append it to **todays_date** using i/o redirection.	9. Displays the UNIX prompt. The **todays_date** file is appended.
10. Use **pr** to format and print the **todays_date** file and pipe the output to the **more** command.	10. Displays the formatted output. Use the **more** command to page through the output.
11. Use the **who** command and append the output to the **who_now** file.	11. Displays the UNIX prompt. The **who_now** file is appended.

WHAT IF IT DOESN'T WORK?

1. Any command that acts upon a file can fail if the file doesn't exist or if you don't have permission to read it. Check for correct spelling of the filename on your command line. Also, use **ls** to check that the file exists and that you're allowed to access it.
2. If there are syntax errors in any command along a UNIX pipeline, then none of the commands will be executed. An error message directs you to the problem. For example, if you accidentally insert a space between the two > symbols when using i/o redirection for appending (>>), the following message appears:

```
syntax error: `>` unexpected
```

Advanced Editing with vi

In Chapter 3 you learned the basics of using the **vi** editor. In this chapter you'll expand your working knowledge of **vi** to use it more effectively. You'll learn about:

- ▲ Operating on words
- ▲ Operating on lines
- ▲ Using line numbers
- ▲ Deleting blocks of text
- ▲ Moving blocks of text
- ▲ Copying blocks of text
- ▲ Substitutions
- ▲ Yank and put
- ▲ Repeating commands
- ▲ Working with other files

Operating on Words

When editing a file you might want to operate on more than a single character at a time. In Chapter 3 you learned how to edit single characters, but **vi** also allows you to work with words. To **vi**, a *word* consists of letters, digits, and an underscored character with blanks or punctuation characters surrounding it. A series of punctuation marks is considered a word. Thus, to **vi,** the string **hello there** consists of two words, while the string **You're** consists of three distinct words: **You, ',** and **re**.

To skip to the beginning of the next word, use the **w** command. Table 7.1 illustrates how to use the **w** command to move from word to word across a line.

Notice that when the next word is on the next line, the **w** command moves the cursor to that line. The **w** command positions the cursor at the beginning of the next word. To position the cursor at the end of the next word, use the **e** command. Compare Tables 7.2 and 7.1. Notice that in Table 7.2, the cursor is positioned at the end, rather than at the beginning, of each word.

Another command, b, moves the cursor backward to the beginning of the previous word, use the **b** command. (Table 7.3).

▼ **Table 7.1. Using the** w **Command**

Before	You Type	After
[B]radley G. Futia		Bradley [G]. Futia
Marion Leach	w	Marion Leach
Cynthia Topfer		Cynthia Topfer
Bradley [G]. Futia		Bradley G[.] Futia
Marion Leach	w	Marion Leach
Cynthia Topfer		Cynthia Topfer
Bradley G[.] Futia		Bradley G. [F]utia
Marion Leach	w	Marion Leach
Cynthia Topfer		Cynthia Topfer
Bradley G. [F]utia		Bradley G. Futia
Marion Leach	w	[M]arion Leach
Cynthia Topfer		Cynthia Topfer

▼ *Table 7.2. Using the e Command*

Before	You Type	After
[B]radley G. Futia		Bradle[y] G. Futia
Marion Leach	e	Marion Leach
Cynthia Topfer		Cynthia Topfer
Bradle[y] G. Futia		Bradley [G]. Futia
Marion Leach	e	Marion Leach
Cynthia Topfer		Cynthia Topfer
Bradley [G]. Futia		Bradley G[.] Futia
Marion Leach	e	Marion Leach
Cynthia Topfer		Cynthia Topfer
Bradley G[.] Futia		Bradley G. Futi[a]
Marion Leach	e	Marion Leach
Cynthia Topfer		Cynthia Topfer

TIP

Rather than issuing a series of w, b, or e commands in order to move
a certain number of words, you can precede any of these commands
with a number that indicates how many words to move. For example, 3w moves the cursor to the third next word.

▼ *Table 7.3. Using the b Command*

Before	You Type	After
Bradley G. Futia		Bradley G. Futia
Marion [L]each	b	[M]arion Leach
Cynthia Topfer		Cynthia Topfer
Bradley G. Futia		Bradley G. [F]utia
[M]arion Leach	b	Marion Leach
Cynthia Topfer		Cynthia Topfer
Bradley G. [F]utia		Bradley G[.] Futia
Marion Leach	b	Marion Leach
Cynthia Topfer		Cynthia Topfer
Bradley G[.] Futia		Bradley [G]. Futia
Marion Leach	b	Marion Leach
Cynthia Topfer		Cynthia Topfer

To delete a group of words, use the **dw** command. Simply position the cursor by issuing one of the word movement commands, and then issue the **dw** command to delete the word. Table 7.4 shows how to combine the **w** and **dw** commands.

To replace a word, use the **cw** command. Position the cursor on the word you want to change, issue the **cw** command, and then type the text with which you wish to replace the word. Press the **Escape** key. Upon issuing the **cw** command, **vi** replaces the last character of the word with a dollar sign ($) to mark the end of the word. Type as much text as you want—even continue with additional lines. When you've entered all the text, press the **Escape** key. Table 7.5 illustrates this command.

CHECK YOURSELF

1. Create a new file containing five lines of text.

2. Position the cursor on the first line and practice moving, one word at a time, to the first character of each word.

3. Practice moving, one word at a time, to the last character of each word.

4. Move backward, one word at a time, to your starting point.

5. Move three words from the current position, then four words, then two words.

6. Delete some words.

7. Change some words.

▼ **Table 7.4. Using the w and dw Commands**

Before	You Type	After
[B]radley G. Futia		Bradley [G]. Futia
Marion Leach	**w**	Marion Leach
Cynthia Topfer		Cynthia Topfer
Bradley [G]. Futia		Bradley [.] Futia
Marion Leach	**dw**	Marion Leach
Cynthia Topfer		Cynthia Topfer
Bradley [.] Futia		Bradley [F]utia
Marion Leach	**dw**	Marion Leach
Cynthia Topfer		Cynthia Topfer

▼ **Table 7.5. Using the *cw* Command**

Before	You Type	After
[B]radley G. Futia		Bradley G. Futia
Marion Leach	**j**	[M]arion Leach
Cynthia Topfer		Cynthia Topfer
Bradley G. Futia		Bradley G. Futia
[M]arion Leach	**cw**	[M]ario$ Leach
Cynthia Topfer		Cynthia Topfer
Bradley G[.] Futia		Bradley G. [F]utia
[M]ario$ Leach	**Hillary**	Hillary[ ]Leach
Cynthia Topfer		Cynthia Topfer
Bradley G. Futia		Bradley G. Futia
Hillary[ ]Leach	**<Esc>**	Hillar[y] Leach
Cynthia Topfer		Cynthia Topfer

ANSWERS

1. Use **vi** and the **a** command to enter five new lines. Press the **Escape** key to return to command mode.

2. Use **k** to move to the first line, then use **h** to move to the first character on that line. Then use the **w** command to move one word at a time across several words.

3. Use the **e** command to move one word at a time across several words.

4. Use the **b** command to move one word at a time back to the first character of the first line.

5. Use **3w**, **4w**, then **2w**.

6. Use **dw** to delete a word.

7. Use **cw** to change a word.

Operating on Lines

Not only does **vi** allow you to manipulate words of text, but it also allows you to manipulate a line of text. Use the dollar sign (**$**) command to position the cursor at the end of the current line. Use the zero (**0**) command to position the cursor at the beginning of the current line. Use the circumflex (**^**) command to position the cursor at the first nonblank character on the current line. Table 7.6 shows all three commands.

There are also commands similar to **cw** and **dw** that operate on lines. Use the **D** command to delete all characters from the current cursor position until the end of the line. Use the **C** command to replace all characters from the current cursor position until the end of the line. As with **cw**, **C** replaces the last character on the line with a dollar sign (**$**) to mark the end of the line. Continue to enter text, and then press the **Escape** key. Table 7.7 illustrates both commands.

To replace part of a line, but not the entire line, use the **R** command. When you issue the **R** command, the characters that you type replace the characters that are on the current line until you press the **Escape** key. Table 7.8 shows an example of using the **R** command.

Use the **G** command to move the cursor to the beginning of the very last line in the file. When preceded by a number, **G** positions the cursor at the beginning of the line whose number is specified. So, **1G** moves you to the first line in the file.

▼ **Table 7.6. Using the Line Movement Commands**

Before	You Type	After
[ ] This is a line.	2w	This [i]s a line.
This [i]s a line.	0	[ ] This is a line.
[ ] This is a line.	$	This is a line.[ ]
This is a line.[ ]	^	[T]his is a line.

CHECK YOURSELF

1. Edit the file created in the last Check Yourself.

2. Position the cursor at the end of the line.

3. Position the cursor at the beginning of the line.

4. Position the cursor at the end of the line.

5. Position the cursor at the first nonblank character of the line.

6. Delete the line.

7. Change the line.

8. Replace some characters on the line.

9. Move to the end of the file.

10. Move to the beginning of the file.

11. Move to the third line of the file.

ANSWERS

1. Enter the **vi** command file by a filename.

2. Use the **$** command.

3. Use the **0** command.

▼ *Table 7.7. Using the D and C Commands*

Before	You Type	After
[T]his is line one.	**w**	This [i]s line one.
This is line two.		This is line two.
This [i]s line one.	**D**	This[ ]
This is line two.		This is line two.
This[ ]	**<Return>**	This
This is line two.		[T]his is line two.
This		This
[T]his is line two.	**C**	[T]his is line two$
This		This
[T]his is line two$	**New Line**	New line[l]ine two$
This		This
New line[l]ine two$	**<Esc>**	New lin[e]

▼ *Table 7.8.* *Using the* R *Command*

Before	You Type	After
[T]his is line one.	R	[T]his is line one.
This is line two.		This is line two.
[T]his is line one.	That	That[ ]is line one.
This is line two.		This is line two.
That[ ]is line one.	<Esc>	Tha[t] is line one.
This is line two.		This is line two.

4. Use the $ command.

5. Use the ^ command.

6. Use the **D** command.

7. Use the **C** command.

8. Use the **R** command.

9. Use the **G** command.

10. Use the **1G** command.

11. Use the **3G** command.

Using Line Numbers

Although scrolling, cursor movement commands, and the editing commands you learned thus far assist in editing single characters or lines, there are other commands that allow you to edit a range of lines in a file. It's neccesary to know the line numbers of the text you're working with when using these commands.

Every line in a file is assigned a *line number* by **vi**. The line numbers aren't visible on the screen, but you can request that **vi** show you a specific line's number. To find out the number of an individual line, first position the cursor on the desired line. Figure 7.1 shows a **vi** screen with the cursor positioned on the line of interest.

▼ *Figure 7.1.* vi *Screen Before Requesting a Line Number*

Howard Bernier	516-555-5555
Jacob S. Leach	813-555-5555
[K]en Kvidahl	908-555-5555
Monica L. Leach	813-555-5551
Jennifer Sukenick	813-555-5554
Marion Leach	908-555-5555
Albert Moshi	212-555-5555
Robert Leach	201-555-5555
Madison Sukenick	813-555-5554

~
~
~
~
~
~
~
~
~
~

To obtain a line number, issue the **^g** command. A line indicating the line number appears at the bottom of the screen. Figure 7.2 shows the result of this command.

To set up your **vi** screen to display line numbers, issue the **:set number** command (Figure 7.3).

Figure 7.4 shows the screen after pressing the **Return** key.

To turn off the line number capability, issue the **:set nonumber**. Line numbers are only made visible by **vi**; they aren't part of the file itself.

Once you have the specific line number, you can use it in combination with commands. Simply enter a colon, the line number, and the command. For example, to "go to" a line, just type a colon, followed by the line number, and then press the **Return** key. Figure 7.5 illustrates a request to "go to" line 3.

Once you press the **Return** key, the cursor moves to the beginning of the line that you requested to "go to" (Figure 7.6).

▼ *Figure 7.2.* vi *Screen After Requesting a Line Number*

Howard Bernier	516-555-5555
Jacob S. Leach	813-555-5555
[K]en Kvidahl	908-555-5555
Monica L. Leach	813-555-5551
Jennifer Sukenick	813-555-5554
Marion Leach	908-555-5555
Albert Moshi	212-555-5555
Robert Leach	201-555-5555
Madison Sukenick	813-555-5554

~

~

~

~

~

~

~

~

~

"phone" line 3 of 9 —33%—

To issue commands for specific lines, position the cursor on the desired line, and then issue the commands. Alternatively, precede the command with the target line number. For example, you can "delete line 2" by issuing a **:2d** command.

To apply a command to a range of lines, enter the two line numbers, separated by a comma; follow with a colon and then the command.

There are also special line number symbols that are useful as well. The dollar sign (**$**) represents the last line in the file. So, to issue a command for the entire file, precede the command with **:1,$**. The period (**.**) represents the current line, the line that the cursor is currently on. So, to issue a command from the current line to the end of the file, simply precede the command with **:.,$**. The next several sections illustrate how to use this capability.

▼ *Figure 7.3.* vi *Screen Before Requesting Line-Number Display*

```
Howard Bernier       516-555-5555
Jacob S. Leach       813-555-5555
[K]en Kvidahl        908-555-5555
Monica L. Leach      813-555-5551
Jennifer Sukenick    813-555-5554
Marion Leach         908-555-5555
Albert Moshi         212-555-5555
Robert Leach         201-555-5555
Madison Sukenick     813-555-5554
~
~
~
~
~
~
~
~
~
:set number[ ]
```

CHECK YOURSELF

1. Edit the file created in the last Check Yourself and add enough text so that there are at least ten lines in the file.

2. Move to a line and obtain its line number.

3. Turn on the line numbering feature of **vi**.

4. Turn off the line numbering feature of **vi**.

5. Go to the fifth line of the file.

6. Delete the third line.

7. Delete the sixth line.

8. Go to the last line.

9. Go to the first line.

▼ *Figure 7.4.* vi *Screen After Requesting Line-Number Display*

```
    1 Howard Bernier        516-555-5555
    2 Jacob S. Leach        813-555-5555
    3 [K]en Kvidahl         908-555-5555
    4 Monica L. Leach       813-555-5551
    5 Jennifer Sukenick     813-555-5554
    6 Marion Leach          908-555-5555
    7 Albert Moshi          212-555-5555
    8 Robert Leach          201-555-5555
    9 Madison Sukenick      813-555-5554
  ~
  ~
  ~
  ~
  ~
  ~
  ~
  ~
  ~
  ~
  :set number
```

ANSWERS

1. Enter the **vi** command file by a filename. If necessary, use **a** to add more lines.

2. Use **k** to move to a line, then use **^g** to obtain the line number.

3. Use **:set number**.

4. Use **:set nonumber**.

5. Use **:5**.

6. Use **:3d**.

7. Use **:6d**.

▼ *Figure 7.5.* vi *Screen Before Requesting to Go to Line 3*

```
Howard Bernier       516-555-5555
Jacob S. Leach       813-555-5555
Ken Kvidahl          908-555-5555
Monica L. Leach      813-555-5551
Jennifer Sukenick    813-555-5554
Marion Leach         908-555-5555
Albert Moshi         212-555-5555
[R]obert Leach       201-555-5555
Madison Sukenick     813-555-5554
~
~
~
~
~
~
~
~
~
~
:3[]
```

8. Use :**$**.

9. Use :**1**.

Deleting Blocks of Text

There are several means by which to delete a block of lines in a file. To delete a small number of consecutive lines in a file, position the cursor at the first line to be deleted, issue the **d** command, and enter the number of lines (including the current line) to delete. This technique is displayed in Table 7.9.

To delete a large number of lines, advance the cursor to the beginning of the group of lines, use **^g** to determine the line number, advance to the end of the group of lines, and use **^g** to obtain that line

▼ *Figure 7.6.* vi *Screen After Requesting to Go to Line 3*

▼ *Figure 7.6.* vi *Screen After Requesting to Go to Line 3*

Howard Bernier	516-555-5555
Jacob S. Leach	813-555-5555
[K]en Kvidahl	908-555-5555
Monica L. Leach	813-555-5551
Jennifer Sukenick	813-555-5554
Marion Leach	908-555-5555
Albert Moshi	212-555-5555
Robert Leach	201-555-5555
Madison Sukenick	813-555-5554

~
~
~
~
~
~
~
~
~
~
:3

number. Enter the line numbers of the first and last lines to be deleted—specify the *range of lines*. Figure 7.7 illustrates this capability. After pressing **Return**, the screen appears like Figure 7.8.

Moving Blocks of Text

Moving a range of lines, or a *block*, is similar to deleting a block. The only differences are that you use the **m** command instead of the **d** command, and that the **m** is followed by a line number that specifies where to move the text. Table 7.10 illustrates how to move lines 2–4 so that they follow line 6.

▼ *Table 7.9. Using the* d *Command to Delete Multiple Lines*

Before	You Type	After
[B]radley G. Futia	**d2 <Return>**	[H]oward Bernier
Marion Leach		Ken Kvidahl
Cynthia Topfer		Monica L. Leach
Howard Bernier		Vincent Futia
Ken Kvidahl		
Monica L. Leach		
Vincent Futia		

▼ *Figure 7.7.* vi *Screen Before Deleting Lines 1–3*

```
        Howard Bernier        516-555-5555
        Jacob S. Leach        813-555-5555
        [K]en Kvidahl         908-555-5555
        Monica L. Leach       813-555-5551
        Jennifer Sukenick     813-555-5554
        Marion Leach          908-555-5555
        Albert Moshi          212-555-5555
        Robert Leach          201-555-5555
        Madison Sukenick      813-555-5554
        ~
        ~
        ~
        ~
        ~
        ~
        ~
        ~
        ~
        :1,3d[]
```

▼ *Figure 7.8.* vi *Screen After Deleting Lines 1–3*

[M]onica L. Leach	813-555-5551
Jennifer Sukenick	813-555-5554
Marion Leach	908-555-5555
Albert Moshi	212-555-5555
Robert Leach	201-555-5555
Madison Sukenick	813-555-5554

~
~
~
~
~
~
~
~
~
~
~
~
~
~

▼ *Table 7.10.* *Using the* m *Command to Move Lines*

Before	You Type	After
[B]radley G. Futia	**:2,4m6 \<Return\>**	[B]radley G. Futia
Marion Leach		Ken Kvidahl
Cynthia Topfer		Monica L. Leach
Howard Bernier		Marion Leach
Ken Kvidahl		Cynthia Topfer
Monica L. Leach		Howard Bernier
Vincent Futia		Vincent Futia

Copying Blocks of Text

Copying blocks of text is accomplished much the same way as moving blocks of text. However, instead of using the **m** command, you use the **t**, or *transpose*, command. A copy of the blocks of text specified by the range of line numbers preceding the **t** is placed after the line number that follows the **t**. Table 7.11 illustrates how to use this command.

CHECK YOURSELF

1. Edit the file created in the last Check Yourself and add enough text so that there are at least ten lines in the file.

2. Delete lines 3–6.

3. Move lines 1 and 2 so that they follow line 4.

4. Copy lines 1 and 2 (the new lines 1 and 2) after line 3.

ANSWERS

1. Enter the **vi** command file by a filename. If necessary, use **a** to add more lines.

2. Use the command line: **:3,6d**.

▼ **Table 7.11. Using the** *t* **Command to Copy Lines**

Before	You Type	After
[B]radley G. Futia	**:2,4t6 <Return>**	[B]radley G. Futia
Marion Leach		Marion Leach
Cynthia Topfer		Cynthia Topfer
Howard Bernier		Howard Bernier
Ken Kvidahl		Ken Kvidahl
Monica L. Leach		Monica L. Leach
Vincent Futia		Marion Leach
		Cynthia Topfer
		Howard Bernier
		Vincent Futia

3. Use the command line: **:1,2m4**.

4. Use the command line: **:1,2t3**.

Substitutions

In Chapter 3 you learned how to search for character strings using **vi**. Another mechanism is to combine searching with a *substitution capability*. To invoke the substitution command, use the **:s** command, specify the pattern to be searched for and the pattern to substitute. Slashes (/) separate the two patterns. Figures 7.9, 7.10, and 7.11 show how to use this command.

When entering the substitution command, keep in mind that it only applies to the line that the cursor is currently on.

▼ **Figure 7.9.** *vi* **Screen Before Entering the Substitution**

```
[H]oward Bernier
Ken Kvidahl
Monica L. Leach
Vincent Futia
~
~
~
~
~
~
~
~
~
~
~
~
~
~
```

▼ *Figure 7.10.* vi *Screen Before Substitution*

```
Howard Bernier
Ken Kvidahl
Monica L. Leach
Vincent Futia
~
~
~
~
~
~
~
~
~
~
~
~
:s/Bernier/The Duck/[ ]
```

Upon pressing **Return**, the substitution command searches for the first occurrence of the specified pattern and then makes a substitution if the pattern is found.

If the pattern specified in the search command isn't found on the current line, then an error message is displayed at the bottom of the screen (Figure 7.12).

This method of using the substitution command only matches the first occurrence of the specified pattern within a line. To invoke the substitution for all occurrences of the pattern within a line, append a **g** (global) to the command. Figures 7.13, 7.14 and 7.15 show how to use global substitution on a line.

Upon pressing **Return**, the substitution command searches for all occurrences of the specified pattern, and then makes substitutions for all occurrences found on the line.

To apply substitutions not only to one line, but to a series of lines in the file, precede the **s** with a range of line numbers (Figures 7.16 and 7.17).

▼ *Figure 7.11.* vi *Screen After Substitution*

```
[H]oward The Duck
Ken Kvidahl
Monica L. Leach
Vincent Futia
~
~
~
~
~
~
~
~
~
~
~
~
~
~
```

Again, the substitution only applies to the first occurrence of the pattern on each line within the specified range.

TIP

To apply the substitution to all occurrences within the range, simply append a g to the command.

CHECK YOURSELF

1. Create a new file of ten lines, with a name on each line (first and last). Make sure that some of the last names are the same.

2. Change the last name of the third person in the file.

3. Change the last name of all of the people in the file, who have the same last name.

4. Change all occurrences of the letter "e" to "a" in lines 4–7.

Substitutions

▼ ***Figure 7.12.*** *vi* ***Screen After Failed Substitution***

```
[H]oward The Duck
Ken Kvidahl
Monica L. Leach
Vincent Futia
~
~
~
~
~
~
~
~
~
~
~
~
~
Substitute pattern match failed
```

ANSWERS

1. Use **vi** and the **a** command to enter ten names. Press **Escape** to return to command mode.

2. Use the command line: **:3s/oldname/newname/**.

3. Use the command line: **:1,$s/oldname/newname/**.

4. Use the command line: **:4,7s/e/a/g**.

Yank and Put

vi offers an alternative method of copying text to other parts of a file by saving the text in a temporary buffer so that you can repeatedly recall it and insert it where you like. The commands that allow you to perform this function are called *yank and put*.

▼ *Figure 7.13.* vi *Screen Before Entering the Substitution*

Howard Bernier
[K]en Kvidahl
Monica L. Leach
Vincent Futia
~
~
~
~
~
~
~
~
~
~
~
~
~
~

To yank a line, position the cursor on the desired line and issue the **yy** command. Nothing appears to have happened, but a copy of the line has been saved and you can recall it using the put command. Move the cursor to the position where you want a copy of the yanked line to appear, and then either use a **p** or **P** command to put the line there. The two forms of the put command are similar to the two forms of the open command (**o** and **O**). The lowercase version, **p**, places the yanked line beneath the current line. And the upper case version, **P**, places the yanked line above the current line. An example of using yank and put with a single line are shown in Table 7.12.

Notice that the put command was applied several times in the example in Table 7.12. The yanked line is available in a buffer so that you can repeatedly put it in multiple positions within a file.

To yank more than one line, move the cursor to the first line of the group of lines that you wish to yank and issue a single **y** along with the number of lines to be yanked (including the current line). Table 7.13 illustrates yanking and putting multiple lines.

▼ *Figure 7.14.* vi *Screen Before the Global Substitution*

```
Howard Bernier
Ken Kvidahl
Monica L. Leach
Vincent Futia
~
~
~
~
~
~
~
~
~
~
~
~
~
:s/K/B/g[ ]
```

Repeating Commands

vi provides a couple of mechanisms for repeating the last command issued. To repeat the last search command (those that start with a / or ?), use the **n** command (for next). To repeat the last editing command—one that changes the contents of the file—use the dot (.) command. You can even use the two in combination. Table 7.14 illustrates both of these commands.

CHECK YOURSELF

1. Edit the file created in the last Check Yourself.

2. Move to the fifth line and obtain a copy of it.

3. Place a copy of the line below line 2.

4. Move to the sixth line and obtain a copy of it.

▼ *Figure 7.15.* vi *Screen After the Global Substitution*

```
Howard The Duck
[B]en Bvidahl
Monica L. Leach
Vincent Futia
~
~
~
~
~
~
~
~
~
~
~
~
~
~
```

5. Place a copy of the line above line 3.

6. Obtain a copy of lines 1–3..

7. Place a copy of these lines after line 6.

8. Search for the first occurrence of the letter "a."

9. Find the next occurrence of the letter "a."

10. Insert the letter "e" after the "a."

11. Search for another "a" and insert another "e" after it.

ANSWERS

1. Enter the **vi** command file by a filename.

2. Use **:5** followed by **yy**.

3. Use **:2** followed by **p**.

▼ *Figure 7.16. vi **Screen Before Requesting A range Substitute***

Repeating
Commands

```
Howard Bernier           516-555-5555
Bradley G. Futia         813-555-5555
Ken Kvidahl              908-555-5555
Monica L. Leach          813-555-5555
Marion Leach             908-555-5555
[C]ynthia Topfer         212-555-5555
Vincent Futia            201-555-5555
~
~
~
~
~
~
~
~
~
~
:2,4s/813/407/[]
```

4. Use **:6** followed by **yy**.

5. Use **:3** followed by **P**.

6. Use **:1** followed by **y2<CR>**.

7. Use **:6** followed by **p**.

8. Use **/a**.

9. Use **n**.

10. Use **a**, type an **e**, followed by **<Esc>..**

11. Use **n** followed by **..**

▼ *Figure 7.17.* vi *Screen After Requesting a Range* *Substitute*

Howard Bernier	516-555-5555
Bradley G. Futia	407-555-5555
Ken Kvidahl	908-555-5555
Monica L. Leach	407-555-5555
Marion Leach	908-555-5555
[C]ynthia Topfer	212-555-5555
Vincent Futia	201-555-5555
~	
~	
~	
~	
~	
~	
~	
~	
~	
~	

Working with Other Files

In Chapter 3 you learned that the **:w** command direct **vi** to write its current text to the file that was named when you invoked the editor. You can also direct **vi** to write to another file by appending a blank and a filename. **vi** takes a snapshot of what you're working on and saves it to the file that you name. Figure 7.18 shows the screen before issuing such a request.

After pressing **Return**, the current working file that **vi** is working on is written to the filename you provide to the **:w** command, **vi** displays a message at the bottom of the screen, and you can continue working with the editor. Figure 7.19 illustrates this command.

There's also a command that lets you read a file into the file you're working on. Simply place the cursor on the line where you would like the contents of a file inserted, issue the **:r** command fol-

▼ *Table 7.12. Using Yank and Put Commands*

Working with Other Files

Before	You Type	After
[T]his is line one.		[T]his is line one.
This is line two.	**yy**	This is line two.
This is line three.		This is line three.
This is line four.		This is line four.
[T]his is line one.		This is line one.
This is line two.	**j**	[T]his is line two.
This is line three.		This is line three.
This is line four.		This is line four.
This is line one.		This is line one.
[T]his is line two.		This is line two.
This is line three.	**p**	[T]his is line one.
This is line four.		This is line three.
		This is line four.
This is line one.		This is line one.
This is line two.		This is line two.
[T]his is line one.	**jj**	This is line one.
This is line three.		This is line three.
This is line four.		[T]his is line four.
This is line one.		This is line one.
This is line two.		This is line two.
This is line one.	**P**	This is line one.
This is line three.		This is line three.
[T]his is line four.		This is line one.
		This is line four.

lowed by the filename, and the contents of that file will be inserted below the current line. Figures 7.20 and 7.21 show how to perform this operation.

Upon pressing **Return**, the named file is read into the the file you're editing and appears below the current cursor position.

CHECK YOURSELF

1. Edit the file created in the last Check Yourself.

2. Add some lines to the file.

3. Save a snapshot of the file.

▼ *Table 7.13. Using Yank and Put with Multiple Lines*

Before	You Type	After
[T]his is line one.		[T]his is line one.
This is line two.	**y1**	This is line two.
This is line three.		This is line three.
This is line four.		This is line four.
[T]his is line one.		This is line one.
This is line two.	**jj**	This is line two.
This is line three.		[T]his is line three.
This is line four.		This is line four.
This is line one.		This is line one.
This is line two.		This is line two.
[T]his is line three.	**p**	This is line three.
This is line four.		[T]his is line one.
		This is line two.
		This is line four.

4. Save a copy of the file to the name **temp**.

5. Read the /**etc/passwd** file into this file.

6. Quit.

ANSWERS

1. Enter the **vi** command file by a filename.

2. Use **a**, enter some lines, hit **<Esc>**.

3. Use **:w**.

4. Use the command line: **:w temp**.

5. Use the command line: **:r /etc/passwd**.

6. Use **:q!**.

▼ *Table 7.14. Repeating Commands*

Before	You Type	After
[T]his is line one.		This is [l]ine one.
This is line two.	/line	This is line two.
This is line three.		This is line three.
This is line four.		This is line four.
This is [l]ine one.		This is line one.
This is line two.	n	This is [l]ine two.
This is line three.		This is line three.
This is line four.		This is line four.
This is line one.		This is line one.
This is [l]ine two.	i	This is [l]ine two.
This is line three.		This is line three.
This is line four.		This is line four.
This is line one.		This is line one.
This is [l]ine two.	my	This is my [l]ine two.
This is line three.		This is line three.
This is line four.		This is line four.
This is line one.		This is line one.
This is my [l]ine two.	<Esc>	This is my[ ]line two.
This is line three.		This is line three.
This is line four.		This is line four.
This is line one.		This is line one.
This is my[ ]line two.	n	This is my [l]ine two.
This is line three.		This is line three.
This is line four.		This is line four.
This is line one.		This is line one.
This is my [l]ine two.	n	This is my line two.
This is line three.		This is [l]ine three.
This is line four.		This is line four.
This is line one.		This is line one.
This is my line two.	.	This is my line two.
This is [l]ine three.		This is my[ ]line three.
This is line four.		This is line four.

▼ *Figure 7.18. Before Writing to a New Filename*

```
Bradley G. Futia
Marion Leach
Cynthia Topfer
Howard Bernier
Ken Kvidahl
Monica L. Leach
Vincent Futia
~
~
~
~
~
~
~
~
~
:w temp_file[ ]
```

QUICK SUMMARY

Command	Description
w	skip to the beginning of the next word
e	skip to the end of the next word
b	skip to the beginning of the previous word
dw	delete word
cw	change word
$	position the cursor at the end of the current line
0	position the cursor at the beginning of the current line
^	position the cursor at the first nonblank character on the current line
D	delete all characters from the current cursor position until the end of the line
C	change all characters from the current cursor position until the end of the line
R	replace characters on the current line until **<Esc>**
G	go to the beginning of the very last line in the file

▼ *Figure 7.19. After Writing to a New Filename*

```
Bradley G. Futia
Marion Leach
Cynthia Topfer
Howard Bernier
Ken Kvidahl
Monica L. Leach
Vincent Futia
~
~
~
~
~
~
~
~
~
~
"temp_file" [New file] 7 lines 102 characters
```

Command	Description
1G	go to the beginning of the very first line in the file
^g	request a line number
:set number	set **vi** number mode on
:set nonumber	set **vi** number mode off
:#	go to line number, where **#** is replaced by a number
:#d	delete line number **#**
:#,@d	delete a range of lines, from line numbers **#** to **@**
:#,@m%	move a range of lines, from line numbers **#** to **@**, to a new position below line number **%**
:#,@t%	transpose (copy) a range of lines, from line numbers **#** to **@** to a new position below line number **%**
:s/aaaa/bbb/	substitute pattern **bbb** for pattern **aaaa**
yy	yank a line
y#	yank current line plus **#** lines below it
p	put line(s) below current line
P	put line(s) above current line
n	repeat last **/** or **?**) command repeat the last editing command

▼ *Figure 7.20. Before Reading a Filename*

Bradley G. Futia
Marion Leach
Cynthia Topfer
[H]oward Bernier
Ken Kvidahl
Monica L. Leach
Vincent Futia
~
~
~
~
~
~
~
~
~
~
:r phone[ ]

Command	Description
:w yyyy	write snapshot to file, **yyyy**
:r yyyy	read file **yyyy** below current line

PRACTICE WHAT YOU'VE LEARNED

This exercise allows you to further modify your **.profile**. Make sure you're in your **home** directory before starting this exercise. Also, notice that part of this exercise asks you to either modify or enter a line concerning a shell variable called **PATH**. The purpose of this variable hasn't been discussed yet, but completing this exercise is a good way to begin practicing with it.

What You Should Do	How the Computer Responds
1. Edit your **.profile** using **vi**.	1. Displays the **vi** screen with your **.profile**.
2. Search for **PS1** using **/PS1**.	2. Positions the cursor **PS1**.

▼ *Figure 7.21. After Reading a File*

```
Bradley G. Futia
Marion Leach
Cynthia Topfer
Howard Bernier
[H]oward Bernier    516-555-5555
Jacob S. Leach      813-555-5555
Ken Kvidahl         908-555-5555
Monica L. Leach     813-555-5551
Jennifer Sukenick   813-555-5554
Marion Leach        908-555-5555
Albert Moshi        212-555-5555
Robert Leach        201-555-5555
Madison Sukenick    813-555-5554
Ken Kvidahl
Monica L. Leach
Vincent Futia
~
~
~
~
```

What You Should Do	How the Computer Responds
3. Use **2w** to move to the value currently assigned to **PS1**.	3. Position the cursor at the first character of the current value for **PS1**.
4. Use **cw** to change the current value.	4. A **$** appears at the end of the word and the characters you type overwrite the current value. Press **<Esc>** when done.

What You Should Do	*How the Computer Responds*
5. Use **/PATH** to search for your **PATH** being set.	5. Position the cursor at the first character, **P**, in **PATH**, or displays a **Pattern not found** message at the bottom of the screen. If there is a **PATH**, proceed to the next step; otherwise, proceed to step 8.
6. Use **w** to position the cursor to the equal sign, =.	6. Position the cursor over the =.
7. Use **a** to append, type **$HOME/Bin:**, followed by <Esc>.	7. Updates the line with what you typed between the = and the remainder of the line. Proceed to step 10.
	8. Enters the line into the file.

WHAT IF IT DOESN'T WORK?

1. If you don't have a **.profile**, the screen goes blank when you execute **vi** and a message at the bottom indicates that this is a new file. Do the Practice What You've Learned exercise from Chapter 3, then proceed with this one.
2. **vi** indicates that you only have read access to the file, or that you're not allowed to write. Check to make sure you're in your **HOME** directory.

Communications

UNIX provides several mechanisms that facilitates communication with other people on your computer system. Some of the tools even extend that communication to people on other machines. In this chapter you'll learn about:

- ▲ **Write and talk**
- ▲ **Electronic mail**
- ▲ **UNIX to UNIX copy**
- ▲ **Call UNIX**
- ▲ **Telnet**
- ▲ **File transfer protocol**
- ▲ **Berkeley r commands**

Write and Talk

write and **talk** are interactive communications programs that allow you to converse with another user on the same system. **write** is a line-oriented communications tool, while **talk** is a screen-oriented tool. Both of these tools require that the person with whom you wish to communicate be logged into the system. You also need to know the login of the person with whom you wish to communicate. You can use **who** to find out who is on the system, and to find the login for the person with whom you wish to communicate.

To use **write**, simply type the command followed by a login as a parameter:

```
$write brad<CR>
```

If **brad** isn't logged on, then write issues a message to that effect and returns you to the UNIX prompt:

```
brad is not logged on.
$
```

If **brad** is logged on, then he receives the following message on his screen:

```
 Message from gwl (tty10) [Sat May 9 15:58:04 ] ...
```

You won't see a response on your screen unless the person with whom you are communicating decides to **write** to you. Type a line and press **Return.** The line is sent to **brad** and it appears on his screen. Continue to send your message, line-by-line, by typing each line and then pressing **Return**. When you're finished, use **^d** to end your message. The following message appears on **brad's** screen, indicating that your communication is complete:

```
<EOT>
```

When another user communicates with you, he or she also issues a **write** command in order to converse with you. So, as each person types a message and presses **Return**, the message appears on the recipient's screen. The screen can get very messy, because people tend to type at different speeds. However, there's a convention for sending messages in an orderly fashion. When you send a message, simply append the character, **o** (over) to the message and wait for a reply from that person that also ends with (**o**). Then proceed to type your reply. When sending your final message, append the **oo** (over and out) to the end of the message; then enter **^d**. The following is a sample of such a conversation:

Write and Talk

```
$write brad<CR>
Hi Brad! (o)<CR>
Message from brad (tty1) [Sat May 9 16:02:37 ] ...
Hi yourself! Whats up? (o)
Want to do lunch? (o)<CR>
Sure, what do you feel like eating? (o)
How about Chinese? (o)<CR>
Great! How about that new place down the street? (o)
Good. Meet you at the elevators at noon, ok? (o)<CR>
OK, I'll be there at noon! (o)
OK, see you then (oo)<CR>
^d
OK (oo)
$
<EOT>
```

talk is a more recent addition to UNIX, and provides the same ability to communicate with other users, but doesn't require the (**o**) convention. **talk** splits the screen into two halves: The bottom half displays what the other person types and the top half displays what you type. Rather than sending a line at a time, as **write** does, the characters are sent to the other person's screen as you type them. To initiate a **talk** session, simply issue the **talk** command and provide the login of the person with whom you wish to talk:

```
$talk brad<CR>
```

The following message appears on **brad**'s terminal:

```
Message from TalkDaemon@alpha
talk: connection requested by gwl@alpha
talk: respond with talk gwl@alpha
```

At this point, **brad** responds by requesting to talk to **gwl**:

```
$talk gwl<CR>
```

This establishes a two-way connection: Both users see the split screen and can type simultaneously. Figure 8.1 shows a typical **talk** screen.

End the talk session with a **^d**. An **<EOT>** message is displayed on the recipient's screen and the UNIX prompt returns.

TIP

If the user with whom you wish to communicate is logged on more than once on a machine, you can talk **or** write **directly to his/her ttyname.**

In addition to providing a more convenient means of communicating than **write**, **talk** supports interactive conversations with users on other machines who are connected to your machine by a network. To talk to someone on another machine, you need to know that person's login and the machine name. To invoke **talk**, use one of the following forms:

```
machine!login
machine.login
```

▼ *Figure 8.1. Typical* talk *Screen*

> **Hi!<CR>**
> **Want to do lunch?<CR>**
> **How about Chinese?<CR>**
> **Good. Meet you at the elevators at noon, ok?<CR>**
> **OK, see you then<CR>**
> **^d**
>
> ---
>
> Hi yourself! What's up?
> Sure, what do you feel like eating?
> Great! How about that new place down the street?
> OK, I'll be there at noon!
> OK
> <EOT>

```
machine:login
login@machine
```

TIP

To disallow other users from interfering with your screen, change the permissions on the file that corresponds to your terminal. The mesg -n **command disallows others from writing to your terminal screen.** mesg -y **turns the permission back on.** mesg **without any arguments reports the permission status for your tty line.**

CHECK YOURSELF

1. Try starting up a conversation with yourself.

2. Type a message to yourself.

3. End the session.

ANSWERS

1. Use **write xxx**, replacing **xxx** with your login.

2. Type a line and press **Return**; the message appears a second time on your screen.

3. Press **^d**, **<EOT>** and the UNIX prompt appears on your screen.

Electronic Mail

Electronic mail (e-mail) is a popular means of communication among computer users. UNIX has supported **e-mail** for a long time. E-mail can be sent to users on different machines, even to users in other parts of the world. Check with your system administrator to find out whether you can send **e-mail** to other machines. If you have your own machine, have knowledge of other UNIX sites, and have a modem, you can establish an electronic link between yourself and others. See the *Operations/System Administration Guide* for more details about setting up such a link.

TIP

Electronic mail isn't the only means of communication available on UNIX. For large systems with many users, UNIX provides the capability to broadcast messages to the entire user population. And, to relay less important information, UNIX provides the news command.

The **mail** command enables you both to send and receive mail. If you have mail, then the following message appears when you login:

```
you have mail
```

To read your mail, simply type **mail**. The first message is printed to the screen, and ends with a **?** prompt. Figure 8.2 displays a short mail message.

The information at the top of the **e-mail** message provides details concerning where the message came from, when it was sent, and when it was received. This information is called the *mail header*. Because UNIX offers a number of different mailing programs, the mail headers may vary in appearance, but the basic information is the same. The prompt at the end of the message allows you to save the mail in a file, delete it, skip over it, and so on. Such commands are listed in Table 8.1.

Only the **d**, **s**, and **w** commands can remove a mail message. If you quit **mail**, the messages remain and you can read them again. The commands **p** and **h** keep the current message on your screen.

▼ *Figure 8.2. Using mail to Read Your Mail*

```
From jake Sat May  9 17:39 EDT 1992
Received: by  alpha
        id AA15688
Date: 9 May 92 17:39:11 EDT (Sat)
From: alpha!jake (Jacob S. Leach)
To: alpha!gwl
Don't forget we have a meeting in Room 101-A at 10AM
Jacob
?
```

To send mail, type the **mail** command, followed by the logins of those to whom you're mailing. **mail** then lets you type your message. If you compose a long message, press **Return** to continue typing. However, once you've pressed **Return**, you can't go back to correct a line. When you're finished entering text, enter either a **^d** or a **.** on a separate line. **mail** sends the message and returns you to the UNIX prompt. For example:

```
$mail jake monica brad hillary<CR>
Don't forget about the department meeting<CR> on
Friday!<CR>
The room is A-202 and the time is 9AM <CR>
sharp!<CR>
It is Jake's turn to bring the donuts!<CR>
^d
$
```

The same message is sent to all four users. For lengthy messages, use **vi** to compose the message in a file. With **vi**, you can correct typing errors. Also, if you have a spell-checker, you can check your spelling and make corrections. To send the file that contains your message, use **mail** and redirect input from the file. For example:

```
$mail jake monica brad hillary < notice<CR>
$
```

Instead of waiting for you to type the mail message, the **mail** command sends the contents of the file, **notice**, to the four users.

▼ *Table 8.1.* mail *Commands*

h	help, list commands
q	quit
p	print current message
s [file]	save to the file
w [file]	same as s, but without headers
d	delete message
-	previous message
+	next message

So far, the mail messages have all been sent to users who are on the same machine as the person sending the mail. There's a different technique for sending mail to a person who is logged on to a different machine. To send mail to a login on a different machine, enter the machine name along with the login. For example, to send mail to **mark**, who is on a machine named **beta**, send it to **beta!mark**. This assumes that your machine knows how to talk to the **beta** machine (again see your system administrator about this).

TIP

If you have logins on more than one machine, you can direct all mail to a single machine. All mail for a given user is stored in a specific file on the system, found in the directory /usr/mail. **The file has the same name as the login. For example,** /usr/mail/gwl. **If you edit the file by inserting the line:** Forward to machine!login, **then any mail sent to you on that machine is forwarded to the machine and login that you specify in the file.**

Many universities, government agencies, standards and user organizations, and corporations have **e-mail** addresses, as well as more advanced mail software that handle addresses like the following:

```
$mail sunLovers@osf.org powerIsOn@gte.com
spysRus@cia.gov < notice<CR>
$
```

These are examples of *internet addresses*. In order to send mail to someone with an internet address, the mail system must be capable of routing the mail so that it reaches its destination. While your system might not be capable of routing, it probably can forward mail to a capable site. Usually, there's at least one *UNIX site* within most metropolitan areas that's capable of routing and is willing to exchange **e-mail** with smaller systems. Check for a local UNIX Users Group in your area to locate such a UNIX site, or get in touch with U UNET, a nonprofit corporation that provides electronic mail services and more. See Appendix D for contact information.

To list the machines with which your machine can communicate, use the **uuname** command. Send a test mail message to **machine!postmaster**.

TIP

When the e-mail connection is made via a dial-up modem, a busy phone, a remote machine being down, or a noisy phone line can delay mail delivery. Chapter 11 teaches you how to monitor remote mail status.

CHECK YOURSELF

1. Send mail to yourself.

2. Read your mail and save it to a file.

3. If there are others on your system, prepare a message in a file, then send it to them.

ANSWERS

1. Type **mail xxxx**, replacing **xxxx** with your login. Type a mail message and end with a **.** typed on a separate line.

2. Type **mail** without any parameters. At the mail prompt (**?**), type **s newmail**. The mail is saved in the file, **newmail**, and the UNIX prompt appears.

3. Use **vi** to create a file that contains the mail message, then send the message to some friends using **mail yyyy zzzz < afile**, replacing **yyyy** and **zzzz** with the logins of your friends. Use **afile** as the filename of the prepared message.

UNIX to UNIX Copy

Not all communications mechanisms are devoted to user-to-user communications. UNIX has facilities that can transfer files between systems. The UNIX to UNIX Copy command, **uucp**, is useful for transferring files between UNIX systems where the only connection is over a serial line—either a directly connected RS-232 cable, or a dial-up link with another machine. Check with your system administrator to find out whether you have such a connection to other machines. If you have your own machine, see the *Operations/System Administration Guide* for more details on how to set up such a link.

uucp works much like **cp** because it's a copy command. Typically, **uucp** either copies a file from your machine to a remote machine, or retrieves a file from a remote machine and copies it to your machine. For example, if you have a HOME directory on the remote machine, **beta**, you can copy a file, using the following command line:

```
$uucp phone beta!$HOME/phone<CR>
$
```

The file is *queued* to be sent to the machine, **beta**, and copied to the filename that you provided for the remote machine. Whether the transfer actually takes place depends upon the same factors that impact the delivery of electronic mail to remote machines.

There are a number of factors that cause **uucp** to fail. If you send a file to a machine name that your system doesn't recognize, then you receive an error message:

```
$uucp phone beta!$HOME/phone<CR>
bad system: beta
uucp failed completely: code -4
$
```

If **uucp** can't find the local file (on the machine that you're logged onto), you receive an error message. However, when copying from a remote machine to your machine, you don't discover problems with remote files until later. **uucp** queues up the job and attempts to copy the file when the dial-up connection is made with the remote machine. Failure results in notification via an **e-mail** message:

```
From uucp Sun May 17 23:10 EDT 1992
>From beta Sun May 17 23:10:34 1992
Received: by alpha
id AA14973; 17 May 92 23:10:34 EDT (Sun)
REQUEST: alpha!/users/gwl/phone ->
beta!/users/gwl/phone (gwl)
(SYSTEM: beta) remote access to path/file denied
Message-Id: <9205172310.AA14973@alpha>
Date: 17 May 92 23:10:34 EDT (Sun)
From: beta@alpha (beta)
To: gwl@alpha
```

Call UNIX

Call UNIX

The Call UNIX, or **cu**, command dials into a remote UNIX machine and lets you login to it from the machine you're currently on. To use the **cu** command, provide the destination as an argument. The destination is a machine name or telephone number. A system name can be used only if your machine is set up with a **uucp** connection to that machine; otherwise, you must use a phone number. For example:

```
$cu beta<CR>
```

At this point, you see a **CONNECTED** message. Press **Break** several times and the login prompt appears. Login on the remote machine, **beta**, in this example.

TIP

You can set up a link between two UNIX machines over a serial line (RS-232 cable) and use cu **to remotely login. See your manuals for more details.**

Alternatively, you can specify the **communications speed** by using the **-s** option, followed by the desired speed. The speed must be a valid parameter for the device(s) being used: 300, 1200, 2400, etc. For example, to dial out on a 9600 baud modem (assuming one is available), enter the following command line:

```
$cu -s9600 5555555<CR>
```

Without this argument, **cu** defaults to the speed of the available device.

When connected to a remote machine, you can transfer files between the two machines. To take a copy of a file from the remote machine while connected via **cu**, use %**take**. Then enter the name of the remote file to be copied, and the name you would like it to be copied to on your local machine:

```
$%take file1 file2<CR>
```

To perform a copy in the opposite direction, from local machine to remote machine, use %**put**:

```
$%put file1 file2<CR>
```

Telnet

telnet is a command that enables you to establish an *interactive session* on a remote machine over a network. To use **telnet**, issue the command, followed by the machine name or the network address of the remote machine with which you wish to establish a connection. The remote machine presents a login prompt:

```
$telnet beta<CR>
Connecting to beta...
Connected to beta
UNIX System V R.4 (beta)
login:
```

If **telnet** is issued without any arguments, a prompt appears, after which you issue **telnet** commands including **open**, **close**, **quit**, **status**, and **?** (for help).

File Transfer Protocol

To transfer files between machines, use the *File Transfer Protocol* (**ftp**) command. Issue **ftp**, followed by a machine name or network address. **ftp** then attempts to establish a connection to the remote machine and presents the **ftp** prompt:

```
$ftp beta<CR>
Connecting to beta...
Connected to beta
ftp>
```

ftp waits for a command, of which there are several. **help** lists the available commands. To get help with a particular command, issue **help**, followed by one of the commands from the list.

The most common commands used with **ftp** are **get** and **put**, to transfer files, **cd**, to change directories, **ls**, to list files, and **bye**, to leave **ftp**. **get** and **put** work much the same way as **%take** and **%put** work with **cu**.

Berkeley r Commands

If you work with a network of UNIX machines, there are a set of commands that help you interact with other machines on the network. They resemble other UNIX commands, but they have the capability to operate over a network. These commands are collectively called the *Berkeley r commands*. The command names are the same as their non-network counterparts but are preceded with an **r**.

TIP

In order for these commands to work properly, set up a special file named .rhosts in your HOME directory. This file contains the names of other machines that you can access over a network. Each entry appears on a line by itself and looks like, machine_name login. For example, if beta monica is in your .rhosts file, it means that monica can access your machine from the beta machine, using any of the r commands.

The **rwho** command works similarly to the **who** command, but **rwho** lists those who are logged onto a *remote* machine. To execute this command, provide it with a remote machine name:

```
$rwho beta<CR>
albert     tty03  Apr 23 10:07
hill       tty05  Apr 22 07:31
gene       tty06  Apr 23 09:30
rob        tty08  Apr 20 09:15
monica     tty09  Apr 23 08:06
brad       tty10  Apr 21 12:46
jake       tty23  Apr 13 07:35
$
```

The **ruptime** command displays status information concerning all of the machines on the same network:

```
$ruptime<CR>
alpha      up 25+07:35, 2 users, load 1.34, 1.05, 0.35
beta       up 2+20:03, 0 users, load 0.00, 0.00, 0.00
```

```
gamma      down 0:03
$
```

The first column displays the machine name, the second column indicates its status, and the third column displays the duration of the status, e.g., the machine **beta**, has been up for 2 days, 20 hours, and 3 minutes, while the machine **gamma**, has been down for 3 minutes. The fourth column shows the number of users that are on the machine, and the final columns indicate the last three load average readings. The higher the number, the more work the machine is performing.

To login to a remote machine, use the **rlogin** command. When followed by a machine name, **rlogin** uses your login to login onto the remote machine:

```
$rlogin beta<CR>
$
```

To copy files between machines, over a network, use the remote copy, **rcp**, command. When a file is located on another machine, precede the pathname with that machine name, followed by a colon (**:**). For example:

```
$rcp phone beta:/b1/gwl/phone<CR>
$
```

You must have permission to write to the remote directory in order to use **rcp**.

To execute a program on another machine, use the remote shell, **rsh**, command. (System V calls the command **remsh**). Enter the command, followed by the remote machine name, and then the command to be executed. For example, to print a file on a remote machine:

```
$remsh beta lp /b1/gwl/phone<CR>
request id is lpb-2436 (1 file)
$
```

By using a pipe, you can print a file that's on your local machine on a remote printer:

```
$cat phone | remsh beta lp<CR>
request id is lpb-2437 (standard input)
$
```

The **phone** file from the local machine is printed, instead of the **phone** file from the remote machine (**beta**).

CHECK YOURSELF

If you've connected to other machines via **uucp** and/or a network, practice using some of the commands that are appropriate for your environment. If you have a single UNIX machine, without network or modem, skip this Check Yourself.

1. Copy a file from your machine to a remote machine.

2. Try to login to a remote machine.

ANSWERS

1. Use **uucp**, **rcp**, or **ftp** to transfer a file.

2. Use **cu**, **telnet**, or **rlogin** to login to a remote machine.

QUICK SUMMARY

Command	Description
write	write messages to a user's screen
talk	two-way, split-screen conversation tool
mail	send and receive electronic mail
news	print news items
uuname	print a list of machines known to this machine
uucp	transfer files between UNIX systems
cu	call another UNIX system
%take	take a file from a remote system (cu)
%put	put a file onto a remote system (cu)
telnet	connect to another machine over a **network**
ftp	transfer a file over a network
rwho	check who is on a remote machine
ruptime	check status of machines on a network
rlogin	remote login over a network
rcp	remote copy over a network

PRACTICE WHAT YOU'VE LEARNED

What You Should Do

1. Use **mail** to send yourself several messages. Send at least five messages by executing **mail xxx** five times, replacing **xxx** with your login.

2. Use **mail** without any arguments to read your mail.

3. Enter an **h** at the prompt.

4. Use **+** to call up the next message.

5. Use **d** to delete the message.

6. Use **-** to move back to the first message.

7. Use **sfilename** to save the message to a file.

8. Use **q** to quit **mail**.

9. Execute **mail** to read the rest of your mail.

How the Computer Responds

1. Displays a blank screen on which to type the message. The UNIX prompt appears after you enter a **.** on a separate line.

2. Displays the first message. The mail prompt, **?**, trails the message.

3. Displays list of valid mail commands, followed by the mail prompt, **?**.

4. Displays the next message followed by the mail prompt, **?**.

5. The message is deleted, and the next message appears on the screen, followed by the mail prompt, **?**.

6. Displays the previous message, followed by the mail prompt, **?**.

7. Writes the message to the named file, and displays the next message, followed by the mail prompt, **?**.

8. Exits the **mail** command and restores the UNIX prompt.

9. Displays another mail message followed by the mail prompt, **?**.

What You Should Do	**How the Computer Responds**
10. Use **d** to delete the message. Repeat this step until the last message is deleted and the UNIX prompt returns.	10. The message is deleted and either another message is displayed or the UNIX prompt returns.

WHAT IF IT DOESN'T WORK?

1. If you fail to send mail to yourself, then you receive a "No mail" message when you issue the **mail** command. Try again.

Simple Shell Programming

You've learned how to enter various UNIX commands at the shell prompt ($), and how to construct command pipelines. You can also program the shell to increase command combination capability. You can construct shell programs, commonly called *shell scripts*, to more easily execute a series of commands. In this chapter you'll learn about:

- ▲ More filters
- ▲ The for command
- ▲ If and test commands
- ▲ Shell scripts
- ▲ Arguments to shell scripts
- ▲ Putting it all together

More Filters

In Chapter 6 you learned about the simple filters, **pr** and **sort**. This section introduces some additional filters. One example is a filter called **tee**. **tee** fits in a pipeline and allows output from a command pass through it to the next command in the pipeline, while copying the output to the files provided as arguments to **tee**. For example, in the following example, **tee** is inserted in the middle of a pipeline to capture the output of the **ls -l** command and save it in the file called **ls_out**. However, the output of the **ls -l** command also flows through the pipeline to the **pr** command:

```
$ls -l | tee ls_out | pr | lp<CR>
request id is lp1-234 (standard input)
$
```

To compare the the unformatted output of the **ls -l** command to the formatted output produced by the **pr** command, insert another **tee** filter between the **pr** command and the **lp** command:

```
$ls -l | tee ls_out | pr | tee pr_out | lp<CR>
request id is lp1-235 (standard input)
$
```

This technique is most useful when you first put together a pipeline to solve a problem. You can examine the input of each command and the output of each command in the pipeline to determine if each is performing the job you expect.

TIP

When using tee, **the contents of the file or files are overwritten. To append the file or files, use the** -a **option:**

```
$ls -l | tee -a ls_out | pr | lp<CR>
```

tee is also used to capture all output written to the screen during a terminal session. To do this, use the **sh** command and pipe the output to **tee**:

```
$sh | tee sh_out<CR>
$
```

In this way, you create a *second shell* (**sh**) that accepts the commands you type. The initial login shell is running the second shell program, (**sh**). The command output not only appears on the screen but is also saved in the file **sh_out**. For example, look at the following sequence of commands:

More Filters

```
$sh | tee sh_out<CR>
$echo Hello! Are you having fun yet?<CR>
Hello! Are you having fun yet?
$date<CR>
Sun Jun 14 08:43:09 EDT 1992
$exit<CR>
$cat sh_out
Hello! Are you having fun yet?
Sun Jun 14 08:43:09 EDT 1992
$
```

There are several points to notice in the example. First, notice that the **exit** command didn't log you off of the system. Instead, it caused the second shell to exit, and returned control to the login shell. Second, notice that **exit** ended the **tee** command that started in the pipeline with the second shell. Now look at the file **sh_out**. Notice that only the output of the commands appears in this file: The **tee** command doesn't capture the input that you typed to the shell.

Used with a pipe, **grep** is a filter that enables you to search for a pattern in one or more files, or in the standard input. When used by itself, **grep** searches for a specific piece of information in a file. For example, to retrieve a person's phone number from a large phone number file:

```
$grep Leach phone<CR>
Monica L. Leach      813-555-5555
Jacob S. Leach       813-555-5555
Marion Leach         908-555-5555
$
```

Alternatively, use a pipeline with two **greps**:

```
$grep Leach phone | grep Jacob<CR>
Jacob S. Leach       813-555-5555
$
```

Notice that the first **grep** is followed by a filename, while the second **grep** isn't. The first **grep** takes its input from the file, extracts all the lines that contain the pattern **Leach** and passes them to the next **grep** through the pipe. The second **grep** takes each line from the pipe and extracts only those lines that contain the pattern **Jacob**. The effect is a two-level filtering process.

As with **echo,** you can use quotes to include multiple words separated by blanks in the search pattern. The pattern must match exactly:

```
$grep 'Jacob S. Leach' phone<CR>
Jacob S. Leach       813-555-5555
$
```

You can also use special characters to devise patterns. For example, if you specify a range of characters within square brackets, then **grep** matches those in the set against a single character. Notice the difference between the following two examples:

```
$grep er phone<CR>
Howard Bernier       516-555-5555
Jennifer Sukenick    813-555-5554
Albert Moshi         212-555-5555
Robert Leach         201-555-5555
$grep [A-Z]er phone<CR>
Howard Bernier       516-555-5555
$
```

[A-Z] only matches one character. Any pattern that started with a capital letter, followed by **er** would have matched this pattern. The next example shows using a set of values:

```
$grep [Bb]er phone<CR>
Howard Bernier       516-555-5555
Albert Moshi         212-555-5555
Robert Leach         201-555-5555
$
```

The patterns **ber** and **Ber** are picked up by **grep.**

egrep offers certain advanced features that **grep** doesn't support. Its most useful capability is to support multiple search patterns, the items of which are separated by the pipe symbol (**|**). The following example illustrates searching for multiple patterns:

```
$egrep 'Monica|Brad|Jacob' phone<CR>
Monica L. Leach      813-555-5555
```

```
Jacob S. Leach       813-555-5555
Bradley G. Futia     407-555-5555
$
```

egrep searches for lines that contain the patterns **Monica**, **Brad**, or **Jacob**.

CHECK YOURSELF

1. Check who is on the system. Capture the output of the **who** command in a file and display it on the screen.

2. Without using the editor, look at your entry in the file, **/etc/passwd**. The **/etc/passwd** file contains your login information.

3. Use **who** and display only the entry corresponding to your login.

ANSWERS

1. Use the command line: **who | tee who_is_on**.

2. Use the command line: **grep gwl /etc/passwd**, replacing **gwl** with your login.

3. Use the command line: **who | grep gwl**, replacing **gwl** with your login.

To extract specific fields from each line of a file or from the standard input, use the filter, **cut**. For example, you can extract only names from the **phone** file. Use the **-c** option, followed by a range of numbers, for example, 1-10, to indicate how many characters to display in each line of input. The following example "cuts" the first 10 characters of each line from the **phone** file:

```
$cut -c1-10 phone<CR>
Howard Ber
Jacob S. L
Ken Kvidah
Monica L.
Jennifer S
Marion Lea
Albert Mos
```

```
Robert Lea
Madison Su
$
```

A wider range of characters must be designated in order to list the names in full. The best way to obtain all of the names, in full, is by counting the number of characters in the longest name in the file. In this case, 17 characters must be "cut" in order to obtain all the names:

```
$cut -c1-17 phone<CR>
Howard Bernier
Jacob S. Leach
Ken Kvidahl
Monica L. Leach
Jennifer Sukenick
Marion Leach
Albert Moshi
Robert Leach
Madison Sukenick
$
```

Now that works! That is, until a name that is longer than 17 characters is added to the **phone** file. This exposes one of the weaknesses of the **-c** option. The **-c** option works well when input in a fixed-size format; that is, when certain data fields are always a constant length. However, if the data's size varies, then you'll use a different option so that you don't have to readjust the ranges you give to **cut**.

cut can be also be inserted into a pipeline to extract specific information from the output of a command:

```
$who | cut -c1-10<CR>
monica
brad
gene
jake
gerald
mark
$
```

Using the **-c** option of **cut** for the output of **who** is a natural fit because the output of **who** always conforms to starting certain fields in specific columns.

To extract multiple ranges of characters, enter the **-c** option, and then list the ranges, separated by commas. For example, to obtain the current month and year, extract two ranges of characters from the output of the **date** command:

```
$date | cut -c5-8,25-28<CR>
Jun 1992
$
```

The first range, 5–8, found the three-character month (Jun) and a blank, while the second range, 25–28, picked up the year (1992). Notice that it's necessary to include a blank character with the month; otherwise, the month and year aren't printed separated by a blank.

There are two **cut** options that work together when there's a *delimiter*, or *separation character*, between data fields. For example, *encrypted passwords* are stored in the **/etc/passwd** file:

```
$cat /etc/passwd<CR>
root:SErP62HFRwKyc:0:0:Super User:/:
monica:3EkL2FUZ5lv5Y:100:100:Monica L. Leach:/users/monica:
gerald:d4e4d8U4S2:108:101:Gerald Topfer:/users/gerald:
hillary:w18hDkIPQPYjU:101:100:Hillary T. Leach:/users/hillary:
brad:w18hDkIPQPYjU:102:100:Bradley G. Futia:/users/brad:
sue:d4ewd8R4S2:103:101:Susan Topfer:/users/sue:
jake:dW2Dw45DW:104:100:Jacob S. Leach:/users/jake:
gwl:R2kbq20J8a6jo:105:100:George W. Leach:/users/gwl:
gene:d3L2e5LcVa2D:106:101:Genevieve Futia:/users/gene:
mark:5TfEd4f6G7k8:107:101:Mark V. Futia:/users/:mark
```

Each field is separated from the next by a colon (**:**). To extract certain fields from such a file, use the **-d** option to enter the delimiter character. Then issue the field, **-f,** option to indicate the fields to display. For example, to extract the logins and names of everyone on the system, extract the first and fifth fields from **/etc/passwd**:

```
$cut -d: -f1,5 /etc/passwd<CR>
root:Super User
monica:Monica L. Leach
gerald:Gerald Topfer
hillary:Hillary T. Leach
brad:Bradley G. Futia
sue:Susan M. Topfer
jake:Jacob S. Leach
gwl:George W. Leach
gene:Genevieve Futia
mark:Mark V. Futia
```

If the fields are separated by tabs, use **cut** with only the **-f** option. If tabs—instead of blanks—are used between the names and phone numbers in the **phone** file, then the following command obtains the names only:

```
$cut -f1 phone<CR>
Howard Bernier
Jacob S. Leach
Ken Kvidahl
Monica L. Leach
Jennifer Sukenick
Marion Leach
Albert Moshi
Robert Leach
Madison Sukenick
$
```

You could try specifying a blank character as the delimiter character, using **-d"**:

```
$cut -d' ' -f1,2 phone<CR>
Howard Bernier
Jacob S.
Ken Kvidahl
Monica L.
```

```
Jennifer Sukenick
Marion Leach
Albert Moshi
Robert Leach
Madison Sukenick
$
```

Notice that in the above output, a last name appeared only for the people who don't have a middle initial. This is the problem with using blanks as the delimiter.

The **paste** command provides the opposite functionality of the **cut** command. To use **paste**, provide it with a list of filenames. **paste** combines lines from these files, separated by tabs. For example, if you have a file called **id_numbers**, which contains one id number per line, then the following procedure extracts an id from the file and combines it with an entry from the **phone** file:

```
$cat id_numbers<CR>
01324
12035
54090
32943
11121
24351
34256
54367
13209
$paste id_numbers phone<CR>
01324    Howard Bernier
12035    Jacob S. Leach
54090    Ken Kvidahl
32943    Monica L. Leach
11121    Jennifer Sukenick
24351    Marion Leach
34256    Albert Moshi
54367    Robert Leach
13209    Madison Sukenick
$
```

CHECK YOURSELF

1. Check who is on the system, but only display their logins.

2. Retrieve your name (not login) from the **/etc/passwd** file.

3. Print the current month, day, and year.

ANSWERS

1. Use the command line: **who | cut -c1-10**.

2. Use the command line: **grep gwl /etc/passwd | cut -d: -f5**, replacing **gwl** with your login.

3. Use the command line: **date | cut -c5-11,25-28**.

The for Command

The UNIX shell is actually a programming language. The shell provides mechanisms with which to repeat a series of commands. Such a programming construct is called *a loop*. The **for** command allows you to perform a series of operations upon a list. The list can consist of filenames, command names, or simply a series of numbers or letters. **for** is executed by typing **for**, followed by a variable name, then the **in** keyword, and then a list. For example:

```
$for i in 1 2 3<CR>
```

In the example, **i** is the variable, and the list consists of the characters **1**, **2**, and **3**.

Upon pressing **Return**, UNIX doesn't display the UNIX prompt ($ in this case), but instead displays a secondary prompt character, usually >. This is because the **for** command is incomplete and the shell expects additional input to complete the execution of the **for** command.

TIP

The secondary prompt character, typically >, is contained in a shell variable called PS2. Similar to the primary UNIX prompt, PS1, the secondary prompt can be changed within a .profile or on the command line.

The line that follows the **for** command contains **do**, and the last line contains **done**. **do** and **done** delimit the beginning and end of the **for** loop. The lines between **do** and **done** indicate the action that takes place. For example, a simple **for** loop is:

```
$for i in 1 2 3<CR>
>do<CR>
> echo hello<CR>
>done<CR>
```

Once you press **Return**, the shell executes the **for** loop. When the loop is complete, the UNIX prompt appears:

```
$for i in 1 2 3<CR>
>do<CR>
> echo hello<CR>
>done<CR>
hello
hello
hello
$
```

The loop is executed once for each of the values, **1, 2,** and **3**. The message is therefore printed three times, once for each item on the list. The list can contain any series of characters, separated by blanks. In addition, the **i** that follows the **for** is a shell variable that contains the current item on the list. You can use the shell variable that follows the **for**—**i** in this case—between the **do** and the **done**, to access the current value that follows the **in**. The following example uses this capability to illustrate how the loop operates:

```
$for i in 1 2 3<CR>
>do<CR>
> echo hello $i<CR>
>done<CR>
hello 1
hello 2
hello 3
$
```

The **for** command is commonly used to execute a series of operations for a list of filenames. For example, to edit a series of files saving their current contents first, move the file to a different name by preceding the filename with **o_**. The filename is stored in the shell variable, **$i**, during each pass through the **for** loop. To change the name, precede the **$i** with **o_**. Pay close attention to the **mv** in the following example:

```
$for i in phone address meetings<CR>
>do<CR>
> mv $i o_$i<CR>
> cp o_$i $i<CR>
> vi $i<CR>
>done<CR>
```

Upon pressing **Return**, the shell variable, **$i**, contains the filename. The **mv** command moves the file from its current name (**$i**) to a new name, **o_$i**. **mv** preserves the date on which the file was last changed. Then **cp** makes a copy back to the original name (**$i**). And finally, the **vi** editor is invoked upon the file. When you exit **vi**, the **for** loop processes the next file in the list. After saving the last file, the loop ends and the UNIX prompt appears.

You can use shell metacharacters rather than a list of files:

```
$for file in Chap*<CR>
>do<CR>
> vi $file<CR>
>done<CR>
```

Using a shell metacharacter produces a list of those filenames that match the specified pattern. The filenames are used, one by one, within the **for** loop. Notice that the following example uses a different name for the shell variable, **file**. You're free to select any name you like.

```
$for file in Chap*<CR>
>do<CR>
> pr $file | lp<CR>
>done<CR>
request id is lp1-236 (standard input)
request id is lp1-237 (standard input)
request id is lp1-238 (standard input)
request id is lp1-239 (standard input)
request id is lp1-240 (standard input)
$
```

The above **for** loop expanded the **Chap***, into a list of five files, each of which is then processed by the command line, **pr $file | lp**.

You can also generate a list by executing a command or command line enclosed within backquotes (`). For example, the following **for** command extracts the entry from the **/etc/passwd** file for each login that's currently logged on:

```
$for id in `who | cut -c1-10`<CR>
>do<CR>
> grep $id /etc/passwd<CR>
>done<CR>
jake:dW2Dw45DW:104:100:Jacob S. Leach:/users/jake:
brad:w18hDkIPQPYjU:102:100:Bradley G. Futia:/users/brad:
sue:d4ewd8R4S2:103:101:Susan Topfer:/users/sue:
$
```

The command line, **who | cut -c1-10**, which is enclosed within backquotes (`), produces a list of logins. This list of logins is then used in the **for** command.

CHECK YOURSELF

1. Use **for** to edit all of your files.

2. Simulate a countdown for lift off of the space shuttle.

3. Produce a list of names—not logins—of the people who are currently on the system.

ANSWERS

1. Use the command line: **for i in *** and invoke **vi $i** within the loop.

2. Use the command line: **for i in 10 9 8 7 6 5 4 3 2 1** and use **$i** to print a message within the loop.

3. Use the command line: **for i in `who | cut -c1-10`** to obtain the logins of the people currently on the system. Within the **for,** use **grep** and **cut** to extract the names from the **/etc/passwd** file.

If and Test Commands

The shell provides a means with which to test values. This is useful for making decisions. For example, you may want to take a different course of action based upon the type of file in a list of files produced by the following **for** command:

```
$for file in *<CR>
```

Some files are ordinary files, while others are directories. Perhaps you want to print a list of ordinary files, but not directories. Combining the **test** and **if** commands can help. The general form of the **if** command is:

```
$if command<CR>
>then<CR>
> commands<CR>
>else<CR>
> commands<CR>
>fi <CR>
```

If the *command* that follows the **if** is successful, then the *commands* that follow the **then** are executed. If the *command* that follows the **if** fails, then the *commands* that follow the **else** are executed.

The **test** command is used to determine the *type of a file*. For example, to test whether a file is a directory, use **test -d**. By preceding the **test** command with an **if**, you can take some action based upon the success or failure of the **test** command:

```
$if test -d Addresses<CR>
>then<CR>
> echo Addresses is a directory!<CR>
>fi<CR>
```

Table 9.1 lists the test command options.

By combining the **for, if**, and **test -f** commands, create a simple command that examines all files in the current directory and prints a message for the ordinary (regular and executable) files:

```
$for file in *<CR>
>do<CR>
> if test -f $file<CR>
> then<CR>
```

▼ **Table 9.1.** *test* **Options**

-d	returns true if file is a directory
-f	returns true if file is a regular file
-r	returns true if file is readable
-w	returns true if file is writable
-x	returns true if file is executable

```
>echo $file is an ordinary file!<CR>
> fi<CR>
>done<CR>
```

Add an **else** case that prints a message to the effect that the file isn't an ordinary file:

```
$for file in *<CR>
>do<CR>
> if test -f $file<CR>
> then<CR>
>echo $file is an ordinary file!<CR>
> else<CR>
>echo $file is not an ordianry file!<CR>
> fi<CR>
>done<CR>
```

You can assemble all of these elements in any fashion you wish in order to perform the desired task. Anywhere that *commands* are allowed, you may insert a **for** or **if** command. For example, there's no reason that you can't put another **if** test after an **else**. Perhaps if the file isn't an ordinary file, but is a directory, you want to print a different message. That can be accomplished with a variation on the above example:

```
$for file in *<CR>
>do<CR>
> if test -f $file<CR>
> then<CR>
>echo $file is an ordinary file!<CR>
> else<CR>
>if test -d $file<CR>
>then<CR>
```

```
>echo $file is a directory!<CR>
>else<CR>
>echo $file is not an ordinary file or directory!<CR>
>fi<CR>
> fi<CR>
>done<CR>
```

CHECK YOURSELF

1. Test all of the files in your home directory and print a message that indicates whether or not they are directories.

2. Test all the files in your home directory and use **lp** to print all ordinary files on the printer.

3. Test all of the files in your home directory, and, if a file is a directory, print a list of all files contained in that directory.

ANSWERS

1. Use the command line: **for i in *** with **if test -d $i**. Print the appropriate message for the **if** part and the **else** part.

2. Use the command line: **for i in *** with **if test -r $i**. Execute the **lp** command for all files that pass the test.

3. Use the command line: **for i in *** with **if test -d $i**. Execute the **ls** command for all files in any directories that pass the test.

Shell Scripts

Shell scripts are shell programs that are stored in files. Using **vi,** you can edit a file and enter a shell program. For example, edit a file called **testfile** and enter the example shell program from the previous section. Then, to execute the shell script, simply type **sh,** followed by the filename:

```
$sh testfile<CR>
```

To execute **testfile,** it must be located in the current directory; otherwise, you must provide **sh** with a full path to the file. This can be annoying, so there's another alternative. Use **chmod** to change the file to an executable file:

```
$ls -l testfile<CR>
-rw-r—- 1 gwl devel 26 May 18 19:28 testfile
$chmod a+x testfile<CR>
$ls -l testfile<CR>
-rwxr-x-r-x 1 gwl devel 26 May 18 19:28 testfile
```

As long as you're in the same directory in which **testfile** resides, you can use the filename as if it were a command. To use **testfile** in any directory, build a **Bin** directory under your home directory, then move **testfile** into that directory. Then, adjust a shell variable called **$PATH** to include this new directory. To look at your **$PATH,** use **echo**:

```
$echo $PATH<CR>
/bin:/usr/bin:.
```

This is the search path that the shell follows to locate a command when you type a command line. Each directory that's searched is separated by a colon (:). The order is significant. In this particular case, the **/bin** is the first directory searched, followed by the **/usr/bin** directory, and then the current directory, indicated by the **..** To insert the **Bin** directory into the **$PATH**, type the following:

```
$PATH=$PATH:$HOME/Bin<CR>
$export PATH <CR>
```

If you forget to type the colon (:), the two directory names run into each other. Also, if you forget to include **$PATH** on the right hand side of the equal sign **(=),** you lose the list of directories that are currently stored in **$PATH**.

Because it's annoying to make these types of changes every time you login, modify your **.profile** by inserting these two lines. Then each time you login, the **$PATH** includes the **Bin** directory, and you can execute the shell scripts that you create and store there.

TIP

An alternative to setting $PATH **and using the** export **command is to use** env. **When used without any arguments,** env **produces a list of current environment variables and their values. To set an environment variable, use** env **followed by the variable, and equal sign (=), and the new value.** env **again displays the current variables and their values. When using** env, **you don't need to use** export.

Arguments to Shell Script

Shell scripts are even more useful because they accept arguments (like UNIX commands). The simplest form of a shell argument is the $0 shell variable. This variable contains the name of the shell script that's currently being executed. The following is an example of a shell script that checks all of the files in a directory and indicates the type of file:

```
for file in *
do
  if test -f $file
  then
    echo $file is an ordinary file!
  else
    if test -d $file
    then
      echo $file is a directory!
      cd $file
      $0
      cd ..
    else
      echo $file is not an ordinary file or directory!
    fi
  fi
done
```

Notice the additional commands that follow the "directory" message:

```
cd $file
$0
cd ..
```

The name of the directory contained in **$file** is used as the argument to **cd** and the shell script changes to that directory. The shell script then invokes another copy of itself to process the files in that directory. The line containing **$0** accomplishes this step. When this new shell completes, the **cd..** is executed. Each instance of this shell script may encounter another directory and cause yet another shell script to be started. This process will stop when there are no more directories to process.

The shell also has other numbered shell variables, for example, **$1**, **$2**, and so on, which match up with arguments that may be passed to a shell script. If you expect always to have a fixed number of arguments passed to a shell script, then you can use these numbered shell variables directly. There's also a shell variable, **$#**, that contains a count of the number of arguments passed to a shell script. You can use this along with an **if test** to determine if the correct number of arguments were passed to the shell script before trying to access them. For example:

```
if test $# = 3
then
 echo First argument is $1
 echo Second argument is $2
 echo Third argument is $3
else
 echo Wrong number of arguments!
fi
```

If you were to use **vi** and create a shell script called **testit** with the above example contained within it, the following examples show how this shell script would react to different numbers of arguments:

```
$testit only two
Wrong number of arguments!
$testit 1 2 3
```

```
First argument is 1
Second argument is 2
Third argument is 3
$testit 1 2 3 4 5
Wrong number of arguments!
```

To modify the behavior of UNIX commands, create a shell script with the same name as a standard UNIX command, place it in your **Bin** directory, and position your **Bin** directory in front of the standard directories in the **$PATH** shell variable. For example, create a "safe" version of the **rm** command so that, before any files are removed, you have an opportunity to change your mind. In order to do this, your version of **rm** must be able to pass along any arguments typed to the real **rm**, should the answer to the question be affirmative. To do this, use the built-in shell variable, **$***. This variable contains all of the arguments passed to the shell script. Examine its use in the following script:

```
echo "Are you sure? (y or n)"
read answer
if test $answer = y
then
 /bin/rm $*
else
 echo no files removed
fi
```

To use this script as your version of rm, use **vi** to put it in a file named **rm**, **chmod a+x** on the file, place it in your **Bin** directory, and make sure that your **Bin** directory is listed ahead of the system directories in the **$PATH** shell variable:

```
$chmod a+x rm
$mv rm $HOME/Bin/rm
$PATH=$HOME/Bin:$PATH
$export PATH
$
```

CHECK YOURSELF

1. Create a **Bin** directory under your **HOME** directory.

2. Set your **PATH** so that it lists this new directory first!

3. Use **vi** to create a file called **rm** in your **Bin** directory. Insert the "safe **rm**"shell script. Don't forget to press **Esc** and then **ZZ** to save it.

4. Set the permissions on this new file so that you can execute it.

5. Create a dummy file called **dumb**.

6. Use your new command to remove the file.

ANSWERS

1. Use the command line: **mkdir $HOME/Bin**.

2. Use the command line: **PATH=$HOME/Bin:$PATH**.

3. Use the command line: **vi $HOME/Bin/rm, a** (for append). Type the shell text . Enter **ZZ** to save it.

4. Use the command line: **chmod 0755 $HOME/Bin/rm**.

5. Use the command line: **cp /etc/passwd dumb**.

6. Use the command line: **rm dumb**.

See Appendix F for suggested reading on shell programming.

QUICK SUMMARY

Command	Description
tee	pipe-fitting, send output to a file and standard output
sh	invoke the shell
grep	pattern matcher
egrep	extended pattern matcher
cut	cut out selected fields
for	looping shell command
if	decision-making shell command
test	test type of file
$PATH	shell environment variable that contains a series of directories

Command	Description
export	make an environment variable visible
env	set/display environment variables
$0	name of the current shell script
$x	an argument passed to a shell script; replace the x with a digit that refers to a specific argument, e.g., 1 for the first, 2 for the second, etc.
$#	special shell variable that contains the number of arguments passed to a shell script
$*	special shell variable that contains a list of all arguments passed to a shell script
read	read a value into a shell variable

PRACTICE WHAT YOU'VE LEARNED

What You Should Do

1. Use **sh | tee holdit** to capture the output from this session.

2. Use **grep** on the /etc/passwd file to extract the entry that corresponds to your login.

3. Use the **for** command to create ten copies of the /etc/passwd file in your **HOME** directory by using **for i in 1 2 3 4 5 6 7 8 9**. Append the value of **$i**. Use the name **tmp_$i**. Copy the file to this name: **cp /etc/passwd tmp_$i**.

4. Use **ls** to verify that the files exist.

5. Use the **for** command to process the odd-numbered files, by using **for i in 1 3 5 7 9**. Change the mode of the files to read-only, e.g., **chmod 0444 tmp_$i**.

How the Computer Responds

1. Displays the UNIX prompt, but all output to the screen is captured in the file **holdit**.

2. Displays the line from the /etc/passwd file that corresponds to your login.

3. When **for** is complete, you see the UNIX prompt.

4. Displays a list of files that includes the ten new files.

5. When **for** is complete, you see the UNIX prompt.

What You Should Do	*How the Computer Responds*
6. Create a **for** command to process all ten files. Within the loop, use the **if** and **test-w** to test whether or not a file in the list is writable. Print a message for both cases.	6. Displays messages that indicate whether or not the files, **tmp_0, tmp_1**, etc. are writable.
7. Use **rm tmp_?** to remove the ten files.	7. When **rm** command is complete, you see the UNIX prompt.
8. Use **ls** to verify that the files were deleted.	8. Displays a list of files. The ten files aren't included.

WHAT IF IT DOESN'T WORK?

1. **grep, for** and other utilities are only as good as the input you provide to them. If you're using shell metacharacters, such as the asterisk *, then there must be files in your current working directory; otherwise the commands won't execute.

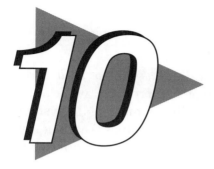

Other Shells
and Tools

In Chapter 9 you learned the basics of shell programming. In addition
to those capabilities, there are other programmable mechanisms that
manipulate data and can be used with the UNIX pipeline concept. This
chapter provides a brief introduction to such mechanisms. In this chapter you'll learn about:

▲ **Shells**

▲ **The C Shell**

▲ **The Korn Shell**

▲ **sed**

▲ **awk**

Shells

The basic UNIX shell, **/bin/sh**, is called *the Bourne Shell* and is named after Steven Bourne who wrote the program while at Bell Labs. But it is not the only shell available on most UNIX systems. There are two other shells called *the C Shell* (**/bin/csh**) and *the Korn Shell* (**/bin/ksh**). There are several ways to determine your default shell. There's the **$SHELL** variable:

```
$echo $SHELL<CR>
/bin/sh
$
```

You can check the **/etc/passwd** file. The last field indicates your login shell:

```
$cat /etc/passwd<CR>
root:SErP62HFRwKyc:0:0:Super User:/:
monica:3EkL2FUZ5lv5Y:100:100:Monica L. Leach:/users/monica:/bin/csh
gerald:d4e4d8U4S2:108:101:Gerald Topfer:/users/gerald:
hillary:w18hDkIPQPYjU:101:100:Hillary T. Leach:/users/hillary:
brad:w18hDkIPQPYjU:102:100:Bradley G. Futia:/users/brad:/bin/ksh
sue:d4ewd8R4S2:103:101:Susan M. Topfer:/users/sue:
jake:dW2Dw45DW:104:100:Jacob S. Leach:/users/jake:/bin/ksh
gwl:R2kbq20J8a6jo:105:100:George W. Leach:/users/gwl:
gene:d3L2e5LcVa2D:106:101:Genevieve Futia:/users/gene:
mark:5TfEd4f6G7k8:107:101:Mark V. Futia:/users/:mark
```

Notice that **monica** runs **csh,** while **brad** and **jake** run **ksh**. The rest of the users have no entry, which means that they run the default shell, or **sh**. At any time, you can change your shell by executing one of the following three commands at the UNIX prompt:

/bin/sh, /bin/csh, or **/bin/ksh**. To permanently change your default shell, the system administrator must adjust your login entry in the **/etc/passwd** file.

UNIX commands are run the same way with all three shells. Pipes, i/o redirection, and shell metacharacters work the same with all three shells. Most of the differences arise when programming the shells and setting shell variables. Also, the C Shell and Korn Shell provide features that the Bourne Shell doesn't support.

The C Shell

The C Shell was developed by Bill Joy, co-founder of Sun Microsystems, while he was a student at the University of California at Berkeley. C Shell first appeared in Berkeley UNIX but has been available on many versions of UNIX for years. It was first introduced into System V with Release 4.0. It was named because some of the programming constructs for looping, decision making, and performing arithmetic resemble those of the C Programming Language. The most popular features are: a history mechanism that remembers the commands you type, and lets you recall, edit, and execute them again; a mechanism that specifies aliases for commands; and a job control capability that helps you place and recall background processes.

Unlike the Bourne Shell's UNIX prompt **($)**, the C Shell's standard prompt is the percent sign (%). The C Shell doesn't use a **.profile** file to configure its behavior; instead, it uses a **.login** file. Furthermore, the C Shell uses a **set** command to assign shell variables, rather than the equal sign (=), used by the Bourne and Korn Shells:

```
$set NAME=George<CR>
$
```

To set C Shell environment variables, use the **setenv** command:

```
$setenv TERM vt100<CR>
$
```

You can set command *aliases* to simplify work. A popular alias is **ll** for **ls -l**:

```
$alias ll ls -l<CR>
$
```

With the C Shell, you can now issue **ll** instead of typing **ls -l**. Typically, you place aliases in the **.login** file in the **HOME** directory so that they are available each time you login.

The exclamation point (!), followed by a number, directs the *command history mechanism* to retrieve a specific command from the **.history** file. To view the current contents of this file, you can type **history**, followed by a blank and a number. The number indicates how far back to go in the **.history** file. For example, **history 4** requests the history mechanism to list the last four commands:

```
$history 4<CR>
5 set NAME=George
6 setenv TERM vt100
7 alias ll ls -l
8 history 4
$
```

Recall the command you want by using its corresponding number:

```
$!5:s/George/Bradley/<CR>
$
```

This command recalls the fifth command from the .**history** file and applies an editing substitution against it (:s/**George/Bradley**/). The result is that the command is re-executed and the shell variable **NAME** is set to **Bradley**. There are additional methods to search for previous commands. For example, to re-execute the last command, simply use **!!**.

Job control allows you to list background processes with the **jobs** command, bring background jobs to the foreground with the **fg** command, send them back into the background with the **bg** command, and kill them with the **kill** command. Jobs placed in the background by using an ampersand at the end of the command line display a job number in square brackets, as well as a pid. The job number, preceded by a percent sign **(%),** can then be used with all of the commands just mentioned. For example:

```
$compress * &<CR>
[1] 342
```

```
$jobs<CR>
[1] Running compress * &
$fg %1<CR>
$
```

This series of commands places the **compress** command in the background, then uses the **jobs** command to view the background jobs, and finally uses the **fg** command to bring the compress job back to the foreground.

The Korn Shell

The Korn Shell is the successor to the Bourne Shell and was developed by David Korn of Bell Labs. It's basically a super-set of the Bourne Shell but provides features similar to the C Shell, such as a history mechanism, aliasing, and job control, as well as some features that the C Shell doesn't provide.

The Korn Shell is backward compatible with the Bourne Shell. The prompt character is the same, it uses the **.profile**, and it uses the same programmable constructs as the Bourne Shell. In fact, if you never use the features that are not found in the Bourne Shell, you would probably not notice that you were running the Korn Shell. Furthermore, since the Korn Shell is also influenced by the C Shell, many of the features that are common to both work similarly, such as job control.

Aliasing, however, works differently in the Korn Shell than it works in the C Shell:

```
$alias ll='ls -l'<CR>
$
```

The Korn Shell offers a number of methods by which to retrieve and edit commands in the **.history** file. The first method is simple, especially to those who are familiar with the **vi** editor. Simply press **Escape**, use the **k** key to move upward to the desired command, then use either the **h** or **l** key to move to the left or right depending on the changes you make. You can use any of the **vi** commands that operate on lines. When you're done, simply press **Return** and the command executes.

TIP

If the vi **method for editing previous commands doesn't work, then use** set -o vi **to turn on** vi.

Job control works similarly in the Korn Shell as it works in the C Shell. The Korn Shell also provides the same programming features as the C Shell but adds support for string manipulation.

CHECK YOURSELF

1. Find out which shell you're currently running.

2. If you're running the Bourne Shell, **/bin/sh**, start up one of the other two shells (assuming you have them).

3. Use a few simple commands.

4. Recall a command or two, using the history mechanism.

5. Exit back to your original shell.

ANSWERS

1. Use **echo $SHELL**.

2. Use either **/bin/csh** or **/bin/ksh**.

3. Use **date, who, cal, echo**.

4. Use **!2** and **!4**.

5. Use **^d**.

sed

To use editing capabilities to make changes to the output of a command or to automatically apply them to a set of files, use the *Stream Editor*, or **sed. sed** is a filter through which to program editing commands so that they can be applied to a list of files or to the standard input.

There are two ways to use **sed**. First, you can set up a command line, placing the editing commands between single quotes:

```
sed 'list of editing commands'
```

Second, you can place the editing commands in a file (typically called the command file) one command per line—and instruct **sed** to take its command input from this file:

```
sed -fcommandfile
```

Either way, supply **sed** with something to work on: the output of a command, piped to **sed,** or with a list of one or more files:

```
who | sed 'list of editing commands'
sed 'list of editing commands' /etc/passwd
```

In both cases, the output of **sed** is sent to standard output. This means that **sed** is ideal for acting as a pipeline filter. You can also use **sed** to operate on a file, by redirecting standard output to a second file. You then have two files: the original file, and the file with the changes applied by **sed**. For example:

```
who | sed 'list of editing commands' | more
```

or

```
sed 'list of editing commands' /etc/passwd > tmp
```

With **sed**, you can use any of the **vi** editing commands that begin with a colon (**:**). The **vi** command most commonly used with **sed** is the pattern substitution command, **:s**. The following example uses pattern substitution to change the area code in the **phone** file:

```
sed 's/212/718/' phone > new_phone
```

sed substitution works in the same way as **vi** substitution. **sed** is applied to each line in the **phone** file, and the new lines are written to the **new_phone** file.

sed is especially useful when making many changes to many files. Rather than using the editor on each file and remembering all of the changes, simply place all of the changes into a file, and use **sed** with the **-f** option. Each edit command from the command file is applied to each line of input that **sed** processes. But be careful: Each edit command changes the line on which the next edit command works.

CHECK YOURSELF

1. Obtain input from **who** and change your login to your first name.

ANSWER

1. Use the command line: **who | grep gwl | sed 's/gwl/ George/'**, replacing **gwl** with your login and **George** with your name.

awk

awk is a programmable, pattern-matching and replacement filter that operates on text. The name combines the first letters of the last names of the three authors: Al Aho, Peter Weinberger, and Brian Kernighan, all of Bell Labs. **awk** is a more powerful tool than **sed**, but it's also more difficult to learn. **sed** works well with simple substitutions, but **awk** provides other capabilities.

awk is a full-fledged programming language. It serves as a *text* application tool, so you wouldn't use it for numeric processing. **awk** is used much the same as **sed;** in fact, the command forms are identical:

awk *'list of awk commands'*

or

awk -f *commandfile*

However, the **awk** editing commands are different from the **sed** editing commands. They look more like *pattern { action }*. For example, to use **awk** to perform the same function as **egrep,** type:

```
who | awk '/gwl/ { print }'
```

awk prints lines of input that match the pattern **gwl**.

Recall from Chapter 9 that **cut** only accommodates character ranges **(-c1-10),** or fields **(-f1,3),** if they're separated by tabs or other characters. **awk** isn't limited in this way. **awk** automatically breaks the input into fields by using tabs or any number of blanks as separators. For example, **awk** counts five fields in the **who** command output:

```
$who<CR>
brad      tty01 Jun 13 10:07
hill      tty02 Jun 13 07:31
alm       tty05 Jun 13 09:30
gene      tty15 Jun 12 06:25
brad      tty06 Jun 13 09:15
monica    tty08 Jun 13 08:06
jacob     tty10 Jun 11 12:46
mark      tty12 Jun 13 07:35
$
```

awk assigns names to each field, much like shell scripts assign shell variables to arguments. **$1** refers to the first field, **$2** to the second, and so on. To inquire about who is on the system and which tty number they're on, you can use **awk** as follows:

```
who | awk '{ print $2, $1}'
tty01 brad
tty02 hill
tty05 alm
tty15 gene
tty06 brad
tty08 monica
tty10 jacob
tty12 mark
```

Because **awk** isn't given a search pattern, every line in the standard input is passed along to the **awk** standard output. However, only those fields that are specified in the **print** appear on the standard output. Notice that the tty numbers are printed first. This is because the printing order of printing is specified to **awk**. You can pass the **awk** output to another command via a pipe:

```
who | awk '{ print $1, $2}' | sort
alm tty05
brad tty01
brad tty06
gene tty15
hill tty02
jacob tty10
mark tty12
monica tty08
```

There are many task that can be accomplished by assembling standard commands and programmable filters with pipes.

CHECK YOURSELF

1. Print a list of who is logged on, and sort the list by the time at which they logged on.

2. Print out a list of who is logged on, and sort the list by the day of the month.

ANSWERS

1. Use the command line: **who | awk '{ print $5, $1}' | sort**

2. Use the command line: **who | awk '{ print $4, $1}' | sort**

QUICK SUMMARY

Command	Description
awk	pattern-matching and processing language
csh	C Shell
ksh	Korn Shell
sed	stream editor

PRACTICE WHAT YOU'VE LEARNED

What You Should Do

1. Use **awk** to extract the filename **($9)**, and time **($8)** from an **ls-l** command.

2. Use **awk** with the output of the **date** command, to extract only the day **($3)**, month **($2)**, and year **($6)**.

3. Execute either **csh** or **ksh**.

How the Computer Responds

1. Displays a list of filenames and times.

2. Displays the date in European format.

3. Displays the appropriate shell prompt (**%** or **$**).

What You Should Do

4. Use either shell **alias** feature to label the command line, **date |** **awk' {print $3, $2, $6}'.** as **eurodate**.

5. Use the alias, **eurodate**, to check the date.

6. Create a similar alias for **curtime**. Set it to, **date |** **awk'{print $4}'**.

7. Execute **curtime**.

8. Use **^d** to exit the shell.

How the Computer Responds

4. The shell accepts the alias and re-displays the shell prompt.

5. Displays the date in European format.

6. The shell accepts the alias and the prompt is displayed.

7. Displays the time.

8. The shell prompt for your normal login shell returns.

WHAT IF IT DOESN'T WORK?

1. **awk** and **sed** are sensitive to syntax errors. Remember to use the single quotes and the curly braces where appropriate.

System Management for Users

If you don't have your own computer, you don't need to know about *system administration*. Most installations have at least one system administrator who manages all of the systems. However, there are certain aspects of system operations that users can monitor and manage. In this chapter you'll learn about:

- ▲ File management
- ▲ Processes management
- ▲ Line printer management
- ▲ Uucp management

File Management

As an individual user, you are restricted to operating upon files in your home directory, or in directories for which you have write permission. The only management you need to consider is removing or compressing files to reduce disk-space consumption in your home directory.

There are two commands that query disk usage; one provides a systemwide view of the disk(s), while the other determines your own, personal usage. The **df** command reports the amount of available disk space that's on the system. Available space is reported in disk blocks, and the number of files that can be created is reported in i-nodes. For example:

```
$df<CR>
/users(/dev/dsk/c2d0s0):6338 blocks 147 i-nodes
/usr(/dev/dsk/c1d0s2):3214 blocks 3082 i-nodes
/(/dev/dsk/c1d0s0):1302 blocks 1123 i-nodes
```

Find the output line from **df** that corresponds to the location of your home directory. If your home directory is located in the /**users** directory, then look at the first line of output in the example.

Disk space is usually measured in 1K (1024) *byte blocks*. The output *number of blocks* indicates how much disk space remains on the system. By finding the device under which your home directory is stored, in the **df** output, you can determine the extent to which your home directory is impacting the available disk space.

An *i-node* is UNIX's internal representation of a file. The number of i-nodes determine the number of files contained in a given file system. If there aren't many i-nodes left, then your ability to create new files is limited.

The **du** command first checks the disk usage in the current directory, and then checks usage for the rest of the directory tree below it. To determine your personal disk usage, move to your home directory, and then issue the **du** command:

```
$pwd<CR>;
/users/gwl;
$ls<CR>;
Bin
Misc
Mail
$du<CR>;
  5./Bin
 23./Misc
285./Mail
314.
```

The output reports the number of disk blocks used within each directory. The **.** directory is the current directory. It displays a cumulative total, including that directory and all subdirectories below it. That's why the numbers don't exactly add up. The current directory uses one disk block.

If there's little disk space left, issue **df** to check the disk, and then **du** to find out how much space you're using. To alleviate the problem, remove files, or to minimize their impact upon disk-usage, compress them. *Compression* is a technique which reduces the amount of disk space that a file requires. However, compressed files are not readable; they must be uncompressed before working with them. On a system in which disk space is limited, it's a good idea to compress files that aren't often used. To do this, use the **compress** command. **compress** takes one or more files as input and outputs compressed versions of those files. The original file(s) are replaced by the compressed versions, and a **.Z** suffix is appended to the compressed files. For example, to compress the **phone** file, use the following command line:

```
$ls -l ph*<CR>
-rw-r--r-- 1 gwl devel 11914 Mar 4 11:05 phone
$compress phone<CR>
$ls -l ph*<CR>
-rw-r--r-- 1 gwl devel 6120 May 17 15:43 phone.Z
```

Notice that the size of the file has been cut in half, from 11914 bytes to 6120 bytes! However, the "cost" is that you can't directly access **phone.Z**. To access the file, issue the **uncompress** command:

```
$ls -l ph*<CR>
-rw-r—r— 1 gwl devel 6120 May 17 15:43 phone.Z
$uncompress phone<CR>
$ls -l ph*<CR>
-rw-r—r— 1 gwl devel 11914 Mar 17 15:45 phone
```

Don't use the **.Z** suffix with the **uncompress** command. The **compress** and **uncompress** commands know when and when not to expect a **.Z**.

CHECK YOURSELF

1. Check disk usage on the system.

2. Check your disk usage.

3. Compress some of your files.

4. Check your disk usage. Notice any difference?

5. Check the system disk usage. Notice any difference?

6. Uncompress your files.

ANSWERS

1. Use **df**.

2. Use **cd** to move to your home directory; then use **du**.

3. Use **compress** *.

4. Use **du**.

5. Use **df**.

6. Use **uncompress** *.

Processes Management

Every command that's issued and every program that's executed on UNIX systems creates one or more *processes* to carry out the work. Even the UNIX shell that manages your login session is a process. UNIX helps you monitor and manage the execution of your processes.

As you've seen, commands are usually executed by typing a command line and then pressing **Return**. However, some commands take a while to complete. Because UNIX is a multiprocessing system, it can execute multiple programs at the same time. To do this, execute commands in what's called *the background*. Ideal candidates for processing in the background are long running commands that don't produce output to the screen. The **compress** command is an excellent choice, especially if you're compressing many files. You can place the **compress** command in the background by appending an ampersand (**&**) to the command line:

```
$compress *&<CR>
1234
$
```

The command is executed in the background, and the UNIX shell prompt appears immediately, rather than appearing after the **compress** command has completed its work. Before the UNIX prompt appears, the *process id (pid) number* (of the **compress** process) appears. Every process is assigned a unique pid by UNIX. The pid helps you monitor and exert control over processes.

Because the **compress** command requires no interactive input from the user, produces no visible output to the screen, and generally takes some time to perform its work, it's an ideal candidate for being put into the background. However, some commands will write to the terminal or require the user to input information via the keyboard. These types of commands should only be placed in the background if i/o redirection is utilized; otherwise, they might interfere with the next command that the user issues. Furthermore, in addition to the standard output and input, there is a third form of standard i/o called *standard error*. Standard error is where any error messages are sent by a process. By default, standard error is written to the terminal just as standard output is. For processes being placed in the background, it is advisable to redirect standard error to a file as well. This can be done by using the output redirection symbol (**>**) prefixed with the digit **2**. Thus, to execute the **ls** command in the background and redirect both standard output and standard error to files, use the following command line:

```
$ls -l > ls_out 2> ls_error&<CR>
1248
$
```

The output of the command, standard out, will be written to the file **ls_out**, while any error messages that are directed by the process to standard error will be written to the file **ls_error**.

TIP

To issue a UNIX command in the background and then logoff, precede the command with nohup. **This command continues the process, even when the hangup signal is received. However, this doesn't work with pipelines, unless the pipeline is placed in a shell script.**

Consider an entire **for** loop—from **for** to **done**—a single command line. This means you can put it in the background using **&**, or redirect input and output. You can also place additional commands after the loop, by following the **done** with a semicolon, **;**, followed by the next command. For example, perhaps you want to make backup copies of all of your files, but if you are copying many files you want to place it in the background. Yet, you may want to alerted when the copying is complete. The following series of commands does the trick:

```
$for file in *<CR>
>do<CR>
>cp$file O_$file<CR>
>done;echo Done! &<CR>
```

When the loop is completed, the **echo** command causes the message **Done!** to be printed. Notice that both the **for** loop and the **echo** command are put into the background. Well, actually that's not true. The **for** loop executes and then the **echo** is put into the background. In order to put both the **for** and the **echo** into the background, both commands must be surrounded by a set of parentheses. Notice the difference:

```
$(for file in *<CR>
>do<CR>
>   cp $file o_$file<CR>
>done;echo Done!) &<CR>
```

The **ps** command checks the process status. When issued without arguments, **ps** produces a list of the executing processes that you own, including the **ps** command itself:

```
$ps<CR>
PID        TTY        TIME       COMMAND
13454      tty19      0:14       sh
14006      tty19      0:00       ps
$
```

In the example, there are two running processes that belong to your login. The first is your login shell, **sh**, and the second is the **ps** command. Notice the PID and COMMAND columns. They identify the processes. The time column indicates execution time. To obtain additional information regarding your processes, execute **ps** with the **-f** option :

```
$ps -f<CR>
```

UID	PID	PPID	C	STIME	TTY	TIME	COMMAND
gwl	13454	1	3	14:17:05	tty19	0:14	-sh
gwl	14006	13454	47	17:10:54	tty19	0:00	ps -f

This option provides: the user id (UID), the parent process id (PPID), the processor utilization (C column), and the starting time (STIME) of the process.
To view all processes on the system, append an -e to the command (ps -ef or ps -e -f).

```
$ps -ef<CR>
```

UID	PID	PPID	C	STIME	TTY	TIME	COMMAND
gwl	13454	1	3	14:17:05	tty19	0:14	-sh
gwl	14006	13454	47	17:10:54	tty19	0:03	ps -f
root	0	0	80	May 22	?	29:12	swapper
root	1	0	0	May 22	?	31:50	/etc/init
brad	7828	1	0	07:28:31	tty21	00:37	-sh
monica	2342	1	3	11:16:25	tty13	0:10	-sh
jake	1365	1	0	09:44:31	tty03	00:24	-sh
root	42	1	0	May 22	?	1:36	/etc/cron
brad	7856	7828	0	07:33:15	tty21	2:04	vi homework
jake	7857	1365	0	07:28:31	tty03	0:12	pr phone
jake	7858	1365	0	07:28:31	tty03	0:02	lp

```
$
```

With this knowledge, you can make decisions regarding processes that aren't performing as expected. Perhaps you executed a command in the background that hasn't completed yet. You can periodically check its progress using **ps**. If you notice that the TIME value isn't increasing, then perhaps the process is stalled. This can happen if you put a command in the background that expects input, but you failed to redirect input. It will sit there and wait. Or you may notice that a process is accumulating a great deal of execution time. It may not be working as expected and can affect system performance. Perhaps another process that has little or no execution time is indicative of a problem. In any event, armed with the process id (PID), you can stop a process owned by you (UID) using the **kill** command:

```
$kill 234<CR>
$
```

The **kill** command sends a signal to process **234**. If the process exists and is owned by you (UID), it's terminated. If you attempt to **kill** a process that you don't own, you receive an error message:

```
$kill 1<CR>
kill: 1: permission denied
$
```

If you attempt to **kill** a process that doesn't exist, you receive the following error message:

```
$kill 50<CR>
kill: 50: no such process
$
```

TIP

Some programs catch these signals and others are programmed to ignore them. If a process doesn't terminate with the kill **command, then use** kill -9. **The** -9 **option to** kill **guarantees a "sure" kill and can only be applied to your processes.**

CHECK YOURSELF

1. Check the processes you're running.

2. Execute **compress** in the background.

3. Get a full listing of your processes.

4. Get a full listing of all processes on the system.

5. When the **compress** process is done, execute **uncompress** in the background.

6. Immediately kill the **uncompress** process.

7. List your files and run **uncompress** on those files that are still compressed. Do this in the foreground.

ANSWERS

1. Use **ps**.

2. Use **compress * &.**

3. Use **ps -f**.

4. Use **ps -ef**.

5. Use **ps** to check the progress of **compress**. When it no longer appears in the list of processes, it's done. Then execute **uncompress * &.**

6. Use **kill -9 ####**, replacing **####** with the pid of the background process.

7. Use **ls**. For those files with a **.Z** suffix, run **uncompress**. Don't include the **.Z**.

Line Printer Management

On systems that have many users who share one or more printers, you might have to wait for a print job to actually be printed. Each printer has an *lp queue* in which print jobs are stored until the printer is available. You can execute **lp** without waiting for the job to actually print.

To monitor the progress of these queues, use the lpstat command. When used without options, **lpstat** shows all print jobs waiting in the queues:

```
$lpstat<CR>
lp1-3746 gwl 6273 May 16 12:20
```

The output of the **lpstat** command indicates that there's only one job waiting on printer lp1. In this example, the lp request id is **lp1-3746**. To remove a job from the print queue, issue the **cancel** command, followed by the lp request id:

```
$cancel lp1-3746<CR>
request "lp1-3746" cancelled
```

If the result of the **lpstat** command indicates that there's a long queue for a particular printer, use the **-p** option to display the printer status:

```
$lpstat -p<CR>
printer lp1 disabled since May 16 12:41 - disabled by
scheduler:
can't open /dev/lp1
printer lp2 is idle. enabled since Aug 14 08:31
printer lp3 is idle. enabled since May 13 09:57
```

The status on printer lp1 indicates that there's a problem with the printer. Perhaps the printer is turned off. Or perhaps a cable is loose. Maybe the printer is out of paper. Check the printer to see if any of these problems are disabling the printer. Correct the situation, then enable printing with the **enable** command:

```
$enable lp1<CR>
printer "lp1" now enabled
```

There's also a **disable** command that deactives the specified printer(s):

```
$disable lp1<CR>
printer "lp1" now disabled
```

disable is useful if you're far away from the printer and want to halt printing. Jobs waiting to print are saved and are automatically printed when the printer is re-enabled, using **enable**.

Uucp Management

Uucp not only refers to the UNIX to UNIX Copy Program, but also to UNIX's dial-up communications protocol. Electronic mail that must be queued for dial-up access to other systems, as well as **uucp** file transfers use this protocol. The **uustat** command allows you to monitor and control the **uucp** queues.

When issued without options, **uustat** displays your outstanding **uucp** jobs:

```
$uustat<CR>
alphaN4dd3    05/16-12:23    S alpha   gwl  1435 /users/gwl/test
alphaC4dd4    05/17-20:56    S alpha   gwl  274 D.jc3b24fb1287
              05/17-20:56    S alpha   gwl  rmail monica
```

Two **uucp** jobs await transfer. The first is a UNIX to UNIX Copy job, and the second is a remote mail (rmail) to **monica**. Notice that the Uucp job only reports one line of status, while the remote mail job reports two. Each status entry begins with an identifier—the destination machine name (**alpha** in this case)—and is followed by a series of letters and digits.

Both jobs are to be transferred to the machine **alpha**. However, the first job has been waiting for over a day. This is a long time and may indicate a problem. To check the status of communications with remote machines, use the -m option:

```
$uustat -m<CR>
sleepy            Locked
grumpy      2C    05/17-20:41 WRONG TIME TO CALL
alpha       2C(2) 05/17-20:56 DEVICE LOCKED
beta              05/17-19:02 SUCCESSFUL
```

Each machine is listed with its status information. The **2C** next to the machines **grumpy** and **alpha** indicates the number of jobs queued up for that machine. If an additional number appears in parentheses, as in the entry for **alpha**, it indicates the number of days that the oldest job has been waiting to go. Also, notice that **sleepy** is locked and that there are no jobs waiting to go. Perhaps something is wrong with the modem. Talk to the system administrator.

To kill any of your **uucp** jobs, use the **uustat** command. To cancel the file transfer, use the **-k** option, followed by the job id:

```
$uustat -k alphaN4dd3<CR>
Job: alphaN4dd3 successfully killed
$
```

CHECK YOURSELF

1. Check the status of all system printers.

2. If any of the printers are idle, then select one and disable it.

3. Send some print jobs to the printer.

4. Check the status of the print jobs.

5. Cancel some of the print jobs, but not all of them.

6. Re-enable the printer so that the remaining jobs will print.

7. Check the status of **uucp** connections to remote machines.

8. Check the status of **uucp** requests.

ANSWERS

1. Use **lpstat -p**.

2. Use **disable lpX**, replacing **lpX** with the name of the printer that's idle.

3. Use **lp -dlpX** to send several print jobs to the printer.

4. Use **lpstat**.

5. Use **cancel,** followed by the lp request ids of the jobs you wish to cancel.

6. Use **enable lpX**.

7. Use **uustat -m.**

8. Use **uustat.**

QUICK SUMMARY

Command	Description
df	free disk space
du	disk usage
compress	compress a file
uncompress	uncompress a file
&	put process in background
nohup	no hangup
ps	process status
kill	kill a process
lpstat	line printer status
cancel	cancel a print job
enable	enable a printer
disable	disable a printer

PRACTICE WHAT YOU'VE LEARNED

What You Should Do

1. Use **ps -ef** to obtain a list of all processes running on the system.
2. Attempt to kill a process for which you are not the owner using **kill -9 xxxx**, replacing **xxxx** with the pid of the process.
3. Execute the **uustat -m** command to discover if your machine can exchange electronic mail with other systems.
4. Select one of the machines listed and send an electronic mail message to the **root** id on that machine.
5. Use **uustat** to check that the mail has been queued.

How the Computer Responds

1. Displays a full list of the running processes on the system.
2. Displays a **permission denied** message.
3. Displays a list of machines and their uucp status.
4. The UNIX prompt appears after the mail is sent.
5. Displays an entry with an **rmail root** entry destined for that machine from you.

What You Should Do	*How the Computer Responds*
6. Kill the mail message using **uustat -kyyyy**, where **yyyy** is the uucp id of the message displayed from the **uustat** output.	6. Displays the message: **Job yyyy successfully killed**.

WHAT IF IT DOESN'T WORK?

1. The **uustat -m** command doesn't produce output if you don't have uucp connections with other machines.
2. If mail is delivered over a network, you might not be able to kill a mail message with **uustat -k**. So compose a nice mail message, because it might be read by someone.

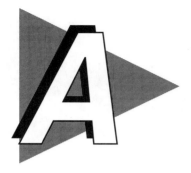

Alphabetical User Command Summary

Command	Description
awk	pattern-matching and processing language
banner	create banners
bc	a calculator
cal	displays a calendar
cancel	cancel a print job
cat	concatenate files
cd	change directory
chgrp	change group
chmod	change mode
chown	change owner
compress	compress a file
cp	copy les
csh	C shell
cu	call another UNIX system
cut	cut out selected fields
date	display the current date and time
df	display free disk space
disable	disable a printer

Command	Description
du	display disk usage
echo	echo arguments to the screen
egrep	extended pattern matcher
enable	enable a printer
env	set/display environment variables
exit	exit from the system
ftp	file transfer over a network
grep	pattern matcher
head	display top of file
kill	kill a process
ksh	Korn shell
lp	line printer
lpstat	line printer status
ls	list files
mail	send and receive electronic mail
mkdir	make a directory
more	page files
mv	move files
news	print news items
nohup	no hangup
passwd	change your password
pg	page files
pr	file formatter
ps	process status
pwd	present working directory
rcp	remote copy over a network
rlogin	remote login over a network
rm	remove files
rmdir	remove directory
rsh	remote execution
ruptime	check status of machines on a network
rwho	check who is on a remote machine
sed	stream editor
sh	invoke the shell
sort	sort utility
tail	display bottom of file
talk	two-way, split-screen conversation tool

Command	Description
tee	pipe-fitting, send output to a file and standard output
telnet	connect to another machine over a network
uncompress	uncompress a file
uucp	transfer files between UNIX systems
uuname	print a list of machines known to this machine
who	see who is on the system
who am i	find out login id you're using
write	write messages to a user's screen

Functional User Command Summary

File Operations

Command	Description
ls	list files
cp	copy files
mv	move files
rm	remove files
cat	concatenate files
more	page files
pg	page files
head	display top of file
tail	display bottom of file
lp	line printer
chmod	change mode
chown	change owner
chgrp	change group

Directory-Only Operations

Command	Description
mkdir	make a directory
cd	change directory
rmdir	remove directory
pwd	print working directory

Filters

Command	Description
pr	file formatter
sort	sort utility
tee	pipe-fitting, send output to a file and standard output
grep	pattern matcher
egrep	extended pattern matcher
cut	cut out selected fields
awk	pattern-matching and processing language
sed	stream editor

Communications

Communications

Command	Description
write	write messages to a user's screen
talk	two-way, split-screen conversation tool
mail	send and receive electronic mail
news	print news items
uuname	print a list of machines known to this machine
uucp	transfer files between UNIX systems
cu	call another UNIX system
telnet	connect to another machine over a network
ftp	file transfer over a network
rwho	check who is on a remote machine
ruptime	check status of machines on a network
rlogin	remote login over a network
rcp	remote copy over a network
rsh	remote execution

System Management

Command	Description
df	free disk space
du	disk usage
compress	compress a file
uncompress	uncompress a file
nohup	no hangup
ps	process status
kill	kill a process
lpstat	line printer status
cancel	cancel a print job
enable	enable a printer
disable	disable a printer

Miscellaneous

Command	Description
passwd	change your password
date	display the current date and time
who	see who is on the system
who am i	find out login id you're using
echo	echo arguments to the screen
banner	create banners
cal	displays a calendar
bc	a calculator
env	set/display environment variables
exit	exit from the system
csh	C shell
ksh	Korn shell
sh	invoke the shell

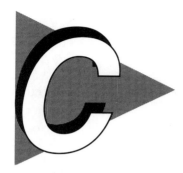

vi Command Summary

The following tables summarize the **vi** commands, grouping them into functional areas:

Cursor Movement

Command	Description
↑ or **k**	move up one line
↓ or **j**	move down one line
← or **h**	move left one character
→ or **l**	move right one character
Backspace	move left one character
Enter	move to the first character of the next line
w	skip to the beginning of the next word

Command	Description
e	skip to the end of the next word
b	skip to the beginning of the previous word

Command	Description
$	position the cursor at the end of the current line
0	position the cursor at the beginning of the current line
^	position the cursor at the first nonblank character on the current line
G	go to the beginning of the very last line in the file
1G	go to the beginning of the very first line in the file
:#	go to line number, where # is replaced with a number

Paging and Scrolling

Command	Description
^f	page forward
^b	page backward
^u	scroll up
^d	scroll down

Adding Text

Command	Description
i	insert before current cursor position
a	append after current cursor position
o	open a line below current line
O	open a line above current line

Deleting Text

Command	Description
x	delete current character
dd	delete current line
dw	delete word
D	delete all characters from the current cursor position until the end of the line
:#d	delete line number #
:#,@d	delete a range of lines, from line numbers # to @

Changing Text

Command	Description
cw	change word
C	change all characters from the current cursor position until the end of the line
R	replace characters on the current line until **Esc**
:s/aaaa/bbb/	substitute pattern bbb for pattern aaaa
.	repeat the last editing command

Copying and Moving Text

Command	Description
:#,@m%	move a range of lines, from line numbers # to @, to a new position below line number %
:#,@t%	transpose (copy) a range of lines, from line numbers # to @, to a new position below line number %
yy	yank a line

Command	Description
y#	yank current line plus # lines below it
p	put line(s) below current line
P	put line(s) above current line

Searching

Command	Description
/	search forward for pattern
?	search backward for pattern
n	repeat last search command

Working with Files

Command	Description
:w	write to the file
:w yyyy	write snapshot to file, yyyy
:r yyyy	read file yyyy below current line

Miscellaneous

Command	Description
Esc	exit insertion mode; switch to command mode
ZZ	save file and exit **vi**
:q	quit **vi**
u	undo last change
^g	request a line number
:set number	set vi number mode on
:set nonumber	set vi number mode off
:set showmode	set vi show mode on
:set noshowmode	set vi show mode off

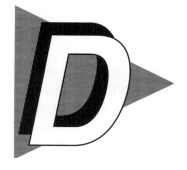

UNIX-Related Organizations

The following organizations are devoted to UNIX and UNIX-like open systems:

USENIX

The USENIX Association is a professional and technical organization devoted to UNIX and UNIX-like open systems. USENIX sponsors two technical conferences each year, one in the winter, the other in the summer, as well as a number of workshops on special topics. USENIX also publishes a bi-monthly newsletter called *;login:* and a quarterly, peer-reviewed journal called *Computing Systems*.

Contact info:

USENIX Association
2560 Ninth Street, Suite 215
Berkeley, CA 94710
Tel. 415-528-8649
office@usenix.org

EurOpen

Formerly the European UNIX Users Group (EUUG), this organization is a loose affiliation of the National UNIX User Groups throughout Europe. There are approximately 20 such groups, including recent additions from the Soviet Union and other Eastern European Nations. Technical conferences are held in the spring and autumn of each year at various locations in Europe. A newsletter is published quarterly.

Contact info:

> EurOpen
> Owles Hall
> Buntingford
> Hertfordshire SG9 9PL
> England
> Tel. +44 763 73039
> Fax. +44 763 73255
> europen@EU.net

UniForum

Formerly called /usr/group, this organization focuses on the UNIX marketplace. A winter conference and trade show is held each year. A newsletter is published bimonthly and a *UNIX Products Directory* is published annually.

Contact info:

> UniForum
> 2901 Tasman Drive
> Suite 201
> Santa Clara, CA 95054
> Tel. 800-255-5620
> Tel. 408-986-8840
> Fax. 408-986-1645

CSRG — Cal Berkeley

CSRG - Cal Berkeley

The Computer Systems Research Group (CSRG) at the University of California, Berkeley is the organization that is responsible for the development of BSD UNIX, which is popular with research institutions and universities.
Contact info:

    Computer Systems Research Group
    Department of Electrical Engineering and Computer Science
    University of California
    Berkeley, CA 94720
    Tel. +1-415-642-7780

UNIX International (UI)

UNIX International (UI) is an industry consortia that was formed not only to support, but also to guide the development of System V.
Contact info:

    UNIX International
    20 Waterview Blvd.
    Parsippany, NJ 07054
    Tel. 201-2638400
    Tel. 800-UI-UNIX-5

Open Software Foundation (OSF)

The Open Software Foundation (OSF) is an industry consortia composed of IBM, DEC, HP/Apollo and other companies. OSF is producing its own version of UNIX, called OSF/1, which makes use of Carnegie-Mellon's Mach OS. The Motif Graphical User Interface is another product of this organization.
Contact info:

    Open Software Foundation
    11 Cambridge Center
    Cambridge, MA 02139
    Tel. +1-617-621-8700
    literature-request@osf.org

UNIX Systems Laboratories (USL)

AT&T transferred the UNIX System V development organization into UNIX Systems Laboratories, Inc. and has sold interest in that venture to other vendors.
Contact info:
UNIX Systems Laboratories, Inc.
190 River Road
Summit, NJ 07901-1400
Tel. 908-522-6000
Tel. 800-828-UNIX

Free Software Foundation

The Free Software Foundation Project GNU (GNU is Not UNIX) is a nonprofit organization devoted to the idea that software should be free. Volunteers develop many useful utilities that are available from a number of sources. The organization's goal is to build an entire UNIX-like operating system. The Free Software Foundation publishes the *GNU Bulletin* twice a year.
Contact info:
Free Software Foundation, Inc.
675 Massachusetts Avenue
Cambridge, MA 02139
617-876-3296
gnu@prep.ai.mit.edu

Other

There are numerous other national and local UNIX Users Groups. For information on groups near you, contact one of the above organizations.

UNIX-Related Publications

The following trade magazines/newspapers are devoted to UNIX:

UNIX Review

UNIX Review is a monthly magazine aimed at the software development community. Free subscriptions are available to qualified individuals.

UNIX Review
600 Harrison Street
San Francisco, CA 94107
Tel. 415-905-2200
[uunet | attmail]!beast!ureview

UNIX WORLD

UNIX WORLD is a monthly magazine.
UNIX WORLD
McGraw-Hill Information Services Company
444 Castro St
Mountain View, CA 94041
Tel. 415-940-1500
ISSN-0739-5922

Open Systems Today

Formerly called *UNIX Today!*, *Open Systems Today* is a biweekly, newspaper-format publication. The main focus is on UNIX-related news items. The newspaper is free to qualified professionals who use UNIX. Paid subscriptions are also available.
Open Systems Today
CMP Publications, Inc.
600 Community Drive
Manhasset, NY 11030
Tel. 516-562-5000
ISSN-1040-5038

Further Reading

This book provides introductory-level knowledge about UNIX. For those who want to learn more, the following is a list of suggested reading, categorized to assist the reader in selecting books from particular areas of interest:

General

Stephen R. Bourne,
The UNIX System V Environment, Second Edition,
Addison-Wesley, 1992.

Kaare Christian and Susan Richter,
The UNIX Operating System, Third Edition,
John Wiley & Sons, 1993.

Don Libes and Sandy Ressler,

Life with UNIX: A Guide for Everyone,
Prentice-Hall, 1989.

Henry McGilton and Rachel Morgan,
Introducing the UNIX System,
McGraw-Hill, 1983.

Mark G. Sobell,
A Practical Guide to the UNIX System V Release 4.0, 2nd Edition,
Benjamin/Cummings, 1991.

UNIX Design

Maurice Bach,
The Design and Implementation of the UNIX Operating System,
Prentice-Hall, 1986.

Sammuel J. Leffler, Marshall Kirk McKusick, Michael J. Karels,
and John S. Quarterman,
*The Design and Implementation of the 4.3BSD UNIX Operating
System,*
Addison-Wesley, 1989.

Andrew Tanenbaum,
Operating Systems: Design and Implementation,
Prentice-Hall, 1987.

Douglas Comer,
Operating System Design: The XINU Approach ,
Prentice-Hall, 1984.

vi

M. I. Bolsky,
The vi User's Handbook,
AT&T, 1984.

Hewlett-Packard,

The Ultimate Guide to the vi and ex Text Editors,
Addison-Wesley, 1989.

William Joy and Mark Horton,
"An Introduction to Display Editing with Vi,"
4.3 Berkeley UNIX Programmer's Manual, 1986.

Linda Lamb,
Learning the vi Editor,
O'Reilly & Associates, Inc., 1991.

Shells and Other Tools

Alfred V. Aho, Brian W. Kernighan, and Peter J. Weinberger,
The AWK Programming Language,
Addison-Wesley, 1988.

Dale Dougherty,
sed & awk,
O'Reilly & Associates, 1991.

Kenneth Ingham,
UNIX Tool Building,
Academic Press, 1991.

Stephen G. Kochan and Patrick H. Wood,
UNIX Shell Programming,
Hayden, 1985.

Ray Swartz,
UNIX Applications Programming: Mastering the Shell,
SAMS, 1990.

System Administration

David Fiedler and Bruce H. Hunter, Revised by Ben Smith,
UNIX System V Release 4 Administration, Second Edition,
SAMS, 1991.

Mike Loukides,

System Performance Tuning,
O'Reilly & Associates, Inc., 1991.

Evi Nemeth, Snyder, and Seebass,
UNIX System Administration Handbook,
Prentice-Hall, 1990.

Tim O'Reilly and Grace Todino,
Managing UUCP and Usenet,
O'Reilly & Associates, Inc., 1991.

Software Development

Brian W. Kernighan and Rob Pike,
The UNIX Programming Environment,
Prentice-Hall, 1984.

Marc J. Rochkind,
Advanced UNIX Programming,
Prentice-Hall, 1985.

UNIX Security

Simson Garfinkel and Gene Spafford,
Practical UNIX Security,
O'Reilly & Associates, Inc., 1991.

Patrick H. Wood and Stephen G. Kochan,
UNIX System Security,
Hayden Book Company, 1985.

Index